150 YEARS OF MAIN LINE
RAILWAYS

150 Years of
Main Line Railways

O. S. NOCK, B.Sc., C.Eng., F.I.C.E., F.I.Mech.E.

DAVID & CHARLES
NEWTON ABBOT   LONDON   NORTH POMFRET (Vt)

British Library Cataloguing in Publication Data

Nock, Oswald Stevens
   150 years of main line railways.
   1. Railroads — Great Britain — History
   I. Hundred and fifty years of main line railways
   385'.0941   HE3018

   ISBN 0-7153-7881-3

Typeset by Trade Linotype Ltd, Birmingham
and printed in Great Britain
by Redwood Burn, Trowbridge
for David & Charles (Publishers) Limited
Brunel House Newton Abbot Devon

Published in the United States of America
by David & Charles Inc
North Pomfret   Vermont 05053   USA

Contents

Preface

The opening of the Liverpool & Manchester Railway 150 years ago can now be seen as one of the really great landmarks in the social history of the human race. In establishing the first inter-city service for passengers in large numbers, it was the starting point for the growth of an entirely new concept of rapid communication between established centres of population, commerce, and industry. It was to add a new dimension to the industrial revolution, which was bringing immense changes to life in Great Britain. The success of the Liverpool & Manchester Railway was absolute. The services it provided soon proved popular, while its shareholders had every reason to be equally satisfied; it is not surprising that many more and longer railways were quickly projected. In the British way of encouraging free enterprise and with an embargo on anything that looked like a monopoly the railway network proliferated until its very prosperity and pre-eminence began to become an embarrassment.

The onset of war in 1914 demanded much closer co-ordination of activities and reduction of duplicated train service facilities. Although this was accepted in the spirit of the emergency which then faced the country, it can, in retrospect, be seen as the first step to what would be needed in the economic crises that followed the grouping of the railways from 1923 onwards. Indeed, while the centenary of the opening of the Liverpool & Manchester Railway was celebrated in 1930 with much colourful pageantry, the railway situation in general was then seriously disquieting. The projectors of other forms of inland transport confidently expected to see railways decline in the near future. The second world war halted talk and aspirations of that kind, but the political events of 1945 and after threw the whole issue into the balance once more, chiefly through the incredibly short-sighted and clumsy way in which the whole transport nationalisation process was handled and driven through Parliament.

The way in which the railways of Britain survived this traumatic period, and another in which their early demise was confidently predicted, is now a matter of history. The 150th anniversary celebrations of the opening of the Liverpool & Manchester Railway are being held not only in a new forward looking atmosphere, but also within an era of magnificent new technological achievement unparalleled since the very early days of railways. To write this book with its inspiriting conclusion has been a very pleasant task, and I should like to express my thanks to the many officers of British Railways and to those of the four main line companies in the grouping period, who between them, over the years, have given me so many opportunities for seeing their manifold activities, both before and behind the scenes.

Twenty Eight,
High Bannerdown,
Batheaston,
Bath.

O. S. Nock
September 1979

CHAPTER 1

The Birth of
Main Line Railways

One hundred and fifty years ago the first link in the network of
main line railways opened between Liverpool and Manchester.
The purist might argue that the Stockton & Darlington had
already been opened, and in operation for five years, and that
one section of it forms part of an important secondary route
today. But the Stockton & Darlington was primarily a local
mineral carrier, and an integral part of existing industry in the
North East. The milestone in its case was the use of steam
locomotives on a line providing public passenger transport.
Actually, so far as passengers were concerned the Stockton &
Darlington in its early days was not greatly different from
earlier railways. Motive power for the coaches was provided by
horses, and the earliest locomotives, of doubtful reliability,
were confined to mineral haulage after that epoch-marking
opening day in September 1825.

The Liverpool & Manchester on the other hand was an
inter-city enterprise — an enterprise to foster travel and trade
between two rapidly growing industrial centres, though as a
point of history neither at that time had attained the status of a
city. The opposition to it was exceedingly diverse. The owners of
the Bridgwater Canal feared that it would take their trade. The
great landowners looked upon it as a grave disturbance to
rural life and organised their tenants and gamekeepers to
obstruct the work of surveyors, while town dwellers and
peasants resorted to violence when confronted with the
prospectors' men. In order to have the Act of Incorporation
passed through Parliament, diversions in the line of route had
to be made to appease hostile landowners, while at first there
was much opposition to the idea of having George Stephenson

as engineer. The most definitive of the early surveys were indeed made by the Rennie brothers, with C. B. Vignoles as a senior assistant.

The route eventually planned and built by George Stephenson followed a remarkably straight course, and in so doing encountered some major difficulties, particularly in cutting directly through the huge sandstone massif of Olive Mount with an excavation having almost vertical sides, and, nearer Manchester, crossing the desolate swamp of Chat Moss. Both these obstacles could have been avoided by route deviations, albeit by increasing the total mileage. It is probable though that construction costs might have been reduced thereby, but the finished work would have been the poorer in the sheer grandeur of construction, and the engineering profession would have been that much poorer in experience. The lessons of Chat Moss were to echo round the world in the history of railway building. The Liverpool & Manchester, moreover, set a pattern in British railway pioneering and construction. It was conceived as an inter-city main line, designed for far higher speeds than any run on the colliery tracks of the North East. It had to be straight, and for the most part easily graded, and the labours involved in Olive Mount cutting, and the line across Chat Moss were essentials that were inevitable.

If the opening of the Liverpool & Manchester Railway, on 15 September 1830, very carefully planned by Joseph Locke, degenerated into utter chaos later in the day, the railway itself soon settled down to good business, and became so profitable that there was a general rush to build more inter-city railways. Six in particular, authorised between 1833 and 1836, are worthy of special notice, in view of the places they eventually took in the ultimate main line network of Great Britain, and of their outstanding importance today. The first was the London & Birmingham, of which Robert Stephenson was the engineer. The success of the Liverpool & Manchester had made invest-ment in railways a very attractive proposition, and in consequence there was no shortage of money when it came to build the London & Birmingham. Robert Stephenson, as a locomotive manufacturer as well as a civil engineer, was sufficiently well aware of the limited tractive ability of steam locomotives then being produced, and even though his line was to pass through the gently rolling countryside of the Chiltern Hills and of Northamptonshire and Warwickshire, he determined that there should be no gradient steeper than 1 in 330 except in the immediate exit from the London terminus where, as at Liverpool, a very steep incline would be operated by cable traction.

Even on the southern part of the line this grading parameter involved him in some colossal engineering works — colossal that is in relation to the experience then existing and the tools that were available; Watford and Kilsby tunnels, the great cuttings at Tring and Roade, and Wolverton embankment could have been largely avoided if the ruling gradient had been around 1 in 200. But it was the philosophy of the Liverpool & Manchester all over again on an altogether vaster scale and in a different terrain. Above all was the overwhelming desire to have a superb road, over which traffic could be operated with the greatest facility. The London & Birmingham, however, was something infinitely more significant for it opened the way from London to the North. Even before the Stockton & Darlington was completed, George Stephenson envisaged a network of railways covering the entire country. His son Robert also had wide vision and to symbolise its grand location as *the* gateway to the North, the terminal station in Euston Grove was dignified by the tremendous Doric Arch.

In the upsurge of railway building enterprise resulting from the success of the Liverpool & Manchester, it was no more than logical that another great project should be launched to link the latter line with the London & Birmingham. In 1833, the Grand Junction was authorised, running from Birmingham to a triangular junction roughly midway between Liverpool and Manchester. To avoid arousing undue opposition, and also of incurring very high costs in land purchase, the London & Birmingham had not penetrated the heart of the latter city any more than it was doing in London; at Birmingham the terminal station was at Curzon Street, at the foot of the hill crowned by the city centre. It was distinguished by another fine classical entrance, which survives. Whatever case might have been made for the demolition of the Doric Arch at Euston in the early 1960s, its destruction was an architectural disaster and one hopes that the lesser but still very fine building at Curzon Street will remain intact.

From its inauguration Curzon Street was shared by both the London & Birmingham and the Grand Junction, and the latter made a complete half circle to the east before proceeding north through Aston. At the outset George Stephenson was engineer and the route was planned to take a direct course to Stafford and Warrington, beyond which lay the T-junction with the Liverpool & Manchester. Like many of the early railways, little regard was paid to the convenience of serving relatively large towns that lay to left and right of the direct route. Thus Walsall, Wolverhampton, Nantwich, Middlewich, and Northwich lay three to five miles on each side. At that time Crewe just did not exist. So far as route planning was concerned, the practice of building lines that were geographically the most direct was quite usual with the early railways in Great Britain. In the case of the Grand Junction the route cut across the lines of existing roads. It would have meant a distinctly roundabout journey by coach, or series of coaches, to get from Stafford to Warrington. At an early stage in the work Joseph Locke succeeded Stephenson as engineer and it was on the Grand Junction that the great association between Locke, as engineer, and Thomas Brassey, as contractor, began. It was a partnership that was to build many thousands of miles of railways.

The next great trunk line to be authorised was the London & Southampton, in 1834, with Francis Giles as engineer. He was well established in the profession and as a fluent speaker he had been employed by the Rennies to oppose George Stephenson's plans for the Liverpool & Manchester Railway. He was a poor organiser and made unfortunate choices for his contractors, and work on the London & Southampton was soon in a muddle. Eventually he had to be relieved of his position and the directors called in Locke to carry on and finish the job. So inaccurate had been the estimates prepared by Giles that after Locke had fully taken the measure of the work, the horrified shareholders were told that the line would cost about £1,700,000 more than the original estimate for the 78 miles of line of between £800,000 and £900,000! Costs apart, the London & Southampton was a beautiful piece of railway, very evenly graded, superbly straight, and capable of becoming a real speedway. The curious point about it though was the choice of Southampton as the south-western terminus.

In 1830, despite its well-nigh unique geographical situation, it was no more than a sleepy old market town, far eclipsed as a seaport by Poole and Portsmouth. Its potential was of course immense, but there seems to have been little regard for it at the time. Because of the difficulties arising from Giles's incompetent handling of the constructional work, the line took a long time to build, and after five years only the first 47 miles, from London to Basingstoke, had been opened to traffic. In that same year of 1839 a branch line was authorised from Bishopstoke, now Eastleigh, to Gosport on the western side of Portsmouth Harbour. This avoided a long detour round the northern reaches of the harbour through Portchester and Cosham, but it meant that the great naval base of Portsmouth received its first railway communication by the back door, as it were. The journey from London had to be completed by ferry across the mouth of the harbour. But the connection was strong enough for the citizens of Portsmouth to object to being served by a branch of the London & Southampton Railway; in the same Act of Parliament by which the Gosport branch was authorised the name of the railway was changed to the London

& South Western. It was opened throughout to Southampton in 1840 and to Gosport in 1842.

The original proposals for the London & Southampton Railway included a very important branch line that was to strike north-west from Basingstoke to Newbury, and follow the eventual route of the Great Western Berks & Hants line to Hungerford and Devizes, thence going on to Bath and Bristol. This, of course, would have been in direct competition with the Great Western, the Bill for which was having a somewhat rough passage through the Parliamentary committees. One would imagine, however, that places of the standing of Bath and Bristol would hardly have appreciated being served by a branch line of a railway called the London & Southampton, and the proposal for this branch was dropped even before the Bill was presented to Parliament. As for the Great Western, from the very outset it stood completely apart from every other railway that had then been proposed or constructed. Apart from the temporary intrusions of men like the Rennies and Francis Giles, all the others had been built by men of what may be termed the Stephenson school—either by George Stephenson himself, his son Robert, or his pupil Joseph Locke. They were hard-headed business propositions built by men who had learned their craft the hard way, and yet with Robert Stephenson and Locke attaining a degree of professionalism that rivalled, where it did not definitely outshine, those who were previously accepted as among the leaders of the engineering profession.

The Great Western appointed Isambard Kingdom Brunel as engineer, and carried along by his own matchless daring and enthusiasm authorised 'the finest work in Britain'. The line was built with the prime object of connecting the port of Bristol with the Capital City, and considerations of intermediate traffic counted for little in the master plan of Brunel. Everything was subsidiary to the aim of getting a straight level route, on which fast running could be made, and in the first 90 miles out of London the only place of any consequence that lay on the direct line was Reading. While the promoters of the London & Southampton had cast eyes towards the old towns of the Kennet Valley—Newbury and Hungerford—and then of proceeding westward through Devizes and Bradford-on-Avon, Brunel ignored the possibilities of a useful intermediate traffic from established, if rural, centres of population, and from Reading headed up the Thames Valley, and westward through the Vale of the White Horse, by-passing old towns like Wallingford and Wantage as, east of Reading, he had by-passed Windsor.

The single-minded grandeur of his conception of a London-Bristol speedway was matched by great elegance in civil engineering, though when it came to the details of the railroad itself and its first rolling stock, Brunel's passion for diving into every detail personally, regardless of any previous experience, made some extensive and not infrequently abortive calls into the deep purse of the company. From its very inception the Great Western gained a reputation for doing things differently from everyone else, but although this characteristic led to many alarming vicissitudes in its long life as an independent company—the longest of all the British railways, from 1835-1947—the nationalised British Railways of today is benefitting from the heritage of Brunel in being able to run one of the fastest express passenger train services in the world westwards from Paddington. His straight, direct line could be adapted readily, with very little in the way of capital cost, for regular running at 125mph, and to enable stations like Swindon and Chippenham to be reached now at start-to-stop average speeds of more than 100mph from London, with correspondingly fast services eastbound.

While this activity in the south was in progress a line authorised as far back as 1829 seemed to be in constant difficulties and in 1835 was far from completion. This was the Newcastle & Carlisle Railway, the first line to be built across Great Britain, virtually from coast to coast. Following the difficulties that had been experienced with the rather primitive steam locomotives on the Stockton & Darlington Railway there had grown up a considerable lobby of opinion that while these new fangled things might be all very well trundling around in collieries up in the North East, they would never be satisfactory on main line railways, and until that same year it was touch and go whether or not the Liverpool & Manchester would be cable-worked. The Newcastle & Carlisle went the whole way, and had a clause in its Act reading: 'No locomotive or moveable steam engine shall be used on the said railway or tram-road for drawing waggons or other carriages, or for any other purpose whatsoever . . .'. And so it was solemnly proposed that this line of 62 miles across the country should be worked entirely by horses! It was fortunate in one respect that the line took so long to build, because it gave time for second thoughts on the subject of motive power, and when the first section was opened, in 1835, between Blaydon and Hexham the company owned two steam locomotives.

The grand opening of the whole line was arranged to take place in 1838, on 18 June, the anniversary of the battle of Waterloo. Apparently the forthcoming event was considered to be as glorious a national occasion as that of 1815 and having locomotives named *Wellington* and *Nelson*, memories of Trafalgar were also combined with it and both carried portraits of the heroes after which they were named. One can thankfully pass over the actual proceedings, which degenerated into a frightful muddle, in which it was long past midnight before the first of the special trains struggled back into Newcastle and the last did not arrive until after 6 am. The Newcastle & Carlisle was one of the prettiest of the early railway routes in Great Britain, following the valley of the Tyne, and, beyond Hexham, passing through beautiful upland country to reach an altitude of 494ft above sea level just before Gilsland. This summit point is unusual in that it is not a peak but the beginning of a completely level plateau six miles long extending to Naworth. It is a section of great historic interest because near Gilsland it crosses the line of the

Roman Wall. West of Naworth the descent is relatively steep. It formed the first railway to enter the City of Carlisle for the great Anglo-Scottish trunk lines came later.

With the London & Birmingham and the Grand Junction on the way to establishment at Curzon Street, it was becoming clear that Birmingham itself was becoming a 'grand junction' of railways in the Midlands, and from it one of the next potentially great lines was authorised in 1836, the Birmingham & Derby. This was really no more than a connecting link to one of George Stephenson's finest works, the North Midland, also authorised in 1836. The North Midland ran from Derby to Leeds, and by its location one can begin to appreciate how the national network envisaged by George Stephenson was beginning to develop. It was planned on easy gradients through Ambergate, Clay Cross and Chesterfield, continuing by what could be termed river-level gradients to Cudworth, and so to Leeds. As Brunel was doing in laying out the Great Western, so George Stephenson followed natural routes which then did not allow deviations to pass through important towns on the side. Sheffield could be reached only by steep gradients and much tunnelling, while to pass through Wakefield would have involved a considerable detour. So they were left out. It was as simple as that! With the completion of the North Midland there was a continuous line of railway from London to Leeds via Birmingham.

There was also a desire to put Leicester on the railway map, and with that object in view the Midland Counties Railway was promoted, with C. B. Vignoles, as engineer. It ran from Derby through Loughborough to Leicester and thence southward to join the London & Birmingham at Rugby. This would provide a much more direct line to the north than that through Birmingham and with the promotion of two more lines, which obtained their Acts in 1836, construction work was soon in hand for a continuous line of railway from London to Tees-side. The two new lines were the York & North Midland, linking with the North Midland proper near Normanton, and the Great North of England, from York to Darlington. They were all relatively easy lines to construct. George Stephenson had some heavy rock and tunnelling work at the southern end of the North Midland, but once Clay Cross was reached the going was fairly smooth. The section south of Clay Cross could have been made a good deal easier had Stephenson adopted a less direct line, and followed the windings of the river Derwent, but the North Midland was laid out for high speed and it was carried straight through all obstructions. In so doing, Stephenson, running somewhat contrary to his usual economical methods, provided the north end of Milford Tunnel, near Duffield, with one of the most unusual and spectacular façades to be seen anywhere in Great Britain, even including those of Brunel on the Great Western.

With the authorisation of this north-easterly group of lines the strategic position of the London & Birmingham and of its terminus at Euston was greatly enhanced, because it was then the starting point of not one, but two trunk routes to the north, and the wisdom of planning the London & Birmingham with an excellent alignment and easy gradients was more than emphasised. Such a route was well equipped to carry heavy traffic. The promotion of the York & North Midland, however, brought into the railway scene a character whose flamboyant personality and questionable tactics did much to usher in the second phase of railway promotion and building, wherein the cautious pioneering of the mid-1830s gave place to a whirlwind of speculation.

CHAPTER 2

Expansion — Maestoso or Mania

The practical difficulties experienced in the building of the early railways, largely self-made by the determination of the engineers to secure the easiest of gradients, led to something of a slump in railway promotion in the late 1830s. The country itself was in a state of great social unrest. The introduction and eventual passage of the first Reform Bill had generated an unparalleled amount of bitterness between classes, and outbreaks of violence were all too frequent. In such conditions those who had capital were not inclined to invest it in projects that were ostensibly so difficult to execute that they were unlikely to become working propositions. Those who hitherto had been foremost in projecting and planning railways were so involved technically in the great works yet unfinished that they had little time for future developments. In this time of uncertainty and lack of enterprise, however, one outstanding personality began to come to the fore, a young linen draper of York named George Hudson.

In the early 1830s the Corporation of York had set up a 'railway committee' to consider proposals for building railways from their city. There had been a scheme for a York & West Riding Railway and Hudson had caused something of a sensation locally by putting his name down for a large majority of the shares in this project. It came to nothing, but it brought Hudson into the public eye and from that time he became the spearhead of all railway promotion in York. In 1835 he met George Stephenson at Whitby and learned of the plans to build the North Midland Railway. It seemed to him that the interests of York would be more quickly and economically served by a link with this great trunk line, which would give

19

them access to a line of continuous railway communication with London. So the York & North Midland Railway was born. Nevertheless, while Hudson's drive and enthusiasm never slackened in the railway slump years from 1837 onwards, in the country generally interest became minimal.

In 1839 the subject of communication with Scotland became a live topic and in August of that year a special Commission of the Board of Trade was appointed to examine existing and possible future systems — not necessarily railways. At that time there were two railway proposals. Hudson and his friends at York naturally favoured a continuation of the line from Darlington and Newcastle to the Border, while London & Birmingham and Grand Junction interests had already asked George Stephenson to look into prospects for a railway to Carlisle. The Commissioners proved non-committal to the extent of obvious lukewarmness. They undoubtedly sensed opinion in the country as a whole, which seemed to take the attitude that it was hardly worth while to have *any* railway communication between England and Scotland. When a new steamer service was put on between Fleetwood and Ardrossan and passengers making rail connections at each end could travel from London to Glasgow in about 24 hours the *Railway Times*, then the financial organ of the railway interest asked: 'What more can any reasonable man want?'

In the Parliamentary session of 1840, not a single railway Bill had been passed and in 1841 there was only one and that for no more than a short branch line. But then there gradually developed a startling and indeed terrifying change. This was due to two principal factors, first that the great trunk lines, already described in chapter 1, had been completed and were earning excellent dividends, and second, that from 1843 the money market in London was in a very easy state. Reserves in the Bank of England were exceptionally high, interest rates were low, and money generally was abundant. Investment in foreign securities had become very unpopular and London stockbrokers, who until this time had left railway shares severely alone, noting that the London & Birmingham, the Grand Junction, and Hudson's York & North Midland were paying 10 per cent dividends, began to look to railway promotion at home as a field for investment.

It was a dangerous situation. Hitherto, railways in England had been promoted and financed by solid commercial men, not primarily as investments but to improve trade and their own business. There was very sound backing, with the assurance that the lines were being built by engineers who made up for what they initially lacked in experience by unquestionable integrity and sense of public duty. But when 'The City' began to take a hand, what started as a genuine move to stir an intensely apathetic money market towards profitable investment, soon swept upwards through a new found enthusiasm into a wild and almost uncontrolled mania. Hudson was very quick to cash in on this situation. He was already empire building on a large scale and in 1844 had engineered the amalgamation of the North Midland, the Midland Counties, and the Derby & Birmingham to form the Midland Railway, the core of one of the greatest British railways of the pre-grouping era. By this amalgamation and his election as first Chairman of the new company, he controlled a route to the north from its junction with the London & Birmingham at Rugby through to York and Darlington.

Before the amalgamation that created the Midland Railway, which Hudson would have effected, mania or not, city men looking for possible fields for railway promotion studied their maps and saw that there was a very large area in eastern England entirely devoid of railways. North of Cambridge, into the counties of Huntingdon, Norfolk and Lincoln, there was not a mile of railway projected, let alone constructed and working. The first proposal for filling this blank on the map was logical enough, a 'direct northern' line, which would start at Cambridge, the most northerly point reached from London by the Northern & Eastern Railway, and would connect the cathedral cities of Ely, Peterborough and Lincoln, and continue northward through Selby to York. There were counter-proposals too and while the 'City' was becoming keenly interested in the promotion of railways, so also were the landed gentry. No longer were gamekeepers instructed to drive off surveyors, smash their instruments and, if necessary, use violence; the great landowners were in many cases in the fore to invest in railways. It was not only a case of getting rich quick. East Anglia and the Fens were peculiarly susceptible to the vagaries of the English climate. In winter, fuel was a great problem. Because of the long, circuitous, and uncertain lines of communication, the price of coal in the 1840s often rose to 50 shillings a ton and in the remoter places it was a positive luxury, quite unattainable by the poorer people. In the worst winter weather, when the canals were frozen, the whole supply system became paralysed and rich and poor shivered alike.

There was much sparring for position. George Hudson may have been glad enough to sponsor lines into Lincolnshire and Norfolk to tap local traffic and feed into his Midland empire, but the proposal for a second, or even a third trunk line from London to the North was not at all to his liking. It would tend to draw through traffic away from Euston and his vital connection with the London & Birmingham at Rugby. At that time, the latter railway was not on the best of terms with its northern associate, the Grand Junction. This suited Hudson's strategy to perfection, because the proposal of a west coast route to Scotland definitely needed the combined backing of both the L&B and the GJ; while those two were at variance, the ground was made clearer for *the* route from England to Scotland to be established on the east coast, via Newcastle and Berwick. At first, however, it was by no means certain that the line to the north would go via Berwick. The Newcastle & Carlisle Railway was then well established and some pressure was exerted to make the crossing of the Tyne at Redheugh, about two miles up stream from the city centre, and use the Newcastle & Carlisle Railway as far as Hexham. There was another ingenious proposal for the 'one' line into Scotland to strike off north from the Newcastle & Carlisle near Gilsland. It would be fed from the west coast side via Carlisle, and from the east coast via Newcastle. But George Stephenson came down like the proverbial ton of bricks against both these proposals, and urged Hudson to settle for the line to Berwick. This took place at the end of 1843.

Several years before, George Stephenson had been consulted about a west coast route into Scotland, and reported that it would be necessary to cross a portion of Morecambe Bay on an embankment, skirt the Cumberland coast to Maryport and there join the already projected Maryport & Carlisle Railway. But in the same year that George Stephenson was making his proposals for a coastal route on easy gradients, Joseph Locke was making a first examination of an inland route through the mountains. He put forward two proposals, the first going up the Lune valley from Lancaster, passing through Kirkby Lonsdale and Sedbergh and tunnelling under the Shap watershed, and the second passing near Kendal. There was another proposal, much favoured in Kendal itself of going through the town, up Long Sleddale, and tunnelling under the Gatesgarth ridge to reach Mardale. This would have been a straighter and easier route to operate, but the tunnel would have been long and probably involved constructional hazards. The promoters, with Locke's concurrence, settled for the route over Shap we know so well today. The Bill was presented to Parliament in November 1843, while the east coast faction were still arguing over their route, and it received the Royal Assent in June 1844. The line between Newcastle and Berwick was authorised a year later.

The Lancaster & Carlisle was a magnificent piece of railway construction, thoroughly typical of everything to which Locke turned his hand. With the rapid improvement in locomotive design and performance, he felt there was no need to go to the expense of a tunnel under the Shap watershed, and built instead the incline that with increasing loads and demand for higher speed proved something of a bugbear for many years to come. In such mountainous country it was inevitable that there should be much curvature, but the alignment was such that until electrification of the line in 1974, no speed restrictions were needed, other than a merely nominal one at Penrith. Now, however, with the enormous potential for speed in modern equipment like the west coast route electric locomotives, the Advanced Passenger Train, and Inter City 125 diesel trains with an ability to climb the steepest gradients at little less than their maximum speeds of 100mph and well over it is another matter, and the curves that have been of no consequence, so far as fast running is concerned, for more than 120 years have become a seriously inhibiting factor. Construction of the original line was pushed ahead with the vigour and efficiency of all Joseph Locke's work and it was opened throughout for traffic in December 1846.

Meanwhile the Bill for the Newcastle & Berwick Railway received the Royal Assent in July 1845. This was entirely a Hudson line and he was soon manoeuvring to amalgamate it not only with the Great North of England and his very own York & North Midland, but also to obtain control by lease of the Newcastle & Carlisle and of the Maryport & Carlisle, thus driving a hostile wedge across the west coast route. While Hudson himself was contriving and manipulating to an unparalleled extent, it can be said that the great majority of the projects with which he was associated were at least practical propositions—which was more than could be said of many of the schemes launched at the height of the Mania. I quote from W. W. Tomlinson's *History of the North Eastern Railway*:

> Besides these schemes already mentioned, there were numerous others, some of them wildly impracticable, which covered the surface of the northern counties in every direction with a complicated network of imaginary lines. The mere enumeration of these lines will show the extraordinary extent to which the North of England was affected

by the railway mania. First in point of order come the trunk lines and extensions of trunk lines: the Newcastle & Leeds Direct Railway from the Northumberland & Lancashire Union Railway at Bishop Auckland via Richmond, Bedale, Masham, Ripon and Ripley to the Leeds & Thirsk Railway at Wath; the Midland & Thirsk Junction Railway from Wakefield through Leeds, Knaresborough and Borough-bridge to Thirsk; the London & Edinburgh, Darlington & Hawick Railway from Darlington by way of Bishop Auckland, Satley, Ebchester and Newbrough to Hawick; the Newcastle-upon-Tyne & Hawick Railway from Hexham up the valleys of the North Tyne and Rede to Hawick; the Newcastle-upon-Tyne, Edinburgh & Direct Glasgow Junction Railway from Newcastle side by side with the Newcastle & Carlisle Railway to Denton Burn, thence by way of Newbiggen House, Belsay, Capheaton, Woodburn, the Rede Valley and Carter Fell to Hawick; the Direct Newcastle-upon-Tyne & Durham & Great North of England Extension Railway from Shincliffe to Gateshead along the Team Valley; the Lancaster & Newcastle-upon-Tyne Direct Railway from Lancaster by the valley of the Lune, Kirkby Lonsdale, Sedbergh, and Kirkby Stephen to Stanhope; the Lancaster & York Railway from Lancaster by way of Settle, Skipton and Knaresborough to York; the York & Kenyon Junction, afterwards the York & East Lancashire Junction Railway from York by Wetherby, Otley, Keighley, Colne, Burnley, Haslingden, Tottington and Tyldesley to the Kenyon Junction of the Liverpool & Manchester Railway; and the most remarkable of all these schemes, the Newcastle & London Coal Railway, an independent line which was to cost five millions and "be devoted exclusively to the con-veyance of coals and goods at a moderate and regular speed".

Hudson was the shrewdest of prospectors, and he realised that among the flood of impracticable and indeed spurious railway schemes there might emerge something solid that would prejudice his interests; in the exciting year of 1847, he attempted to secure control of the North British Railway and thus put himself in supreme command from Rugby to Edinburgh. The line then bearing the name of North British was only that extending from Edinburgh to Berwick. It had been opened in 1846, and in 1847 Hudson, who was a director, offered to take a lease of it at eight per cent of the share capital. Such a wild proliferation of railways were then being promoted, however, that the lessees should have the option of terminating the lease at the end of every three years, on giving one year's notice. A potential rival was the projected Newcastle-upon-Tyne, Edinburgh & direct Glasgow Junction Railway. But though Hudson's offer gave the North British the right to amalgamate with his English companies on equal terms, if the lease were terminated, the North British rejected his offer. The Newcastle-Berwick section was opened in 1850 with the completion of the Royal Border Bridge over the Tweed. There was then continuous rail communication from London to Edinburgh, still of course starting from Euston.

The men of the Grand Junction, who had strongly influenced and supported the building of the Lancaster & Carlisle Railway, had no intention of letting the west coast line to the north end short of the Border, and as early as 1836 its engineer, Joseph Locke, had travelled into Scotland to make some preliminary surveys of possible routes to the north. His recommendation to make a line up Annandale and then up from Beattock to the head waters of the Clyde aroused fierce antagonism. It was argued that not only did this route involve very severe gradients but that it by-passed the principal centres of population, Dumfries, the towns of Nithsdale, and Kilmarnock. But Locke and his Grand Junction sponsors were thinking in far broader terms than a line merely from Carlisle to Glasgow. Had that been the sole aim the Nithsdale route was obviously the better. Entering the industrial lowland belt of Scotland from Upper Clydesdale, however, put them in a far stronger strategic position for a much wider development.

On reaching Carstairs, for example, they would be as favourably placed for an approach to Edinburgh, as to Glasgow, while a middle route leading further north opened the way to Perth, Dundee and Aberdeen.

The fact that the new railway had been inspired by English interests counted against it in Scotland, but promoted as the Caledonian Railway it won through to Royal Assent in July 1845 and a façade of impartiality was presented by a three-pronged cutting of the first turf, at Carstairs—one towards Glasgow, one towards Edinburgh and one towards Carlisle. With that incomparable partnership of Locke as Engineer and Thomas Brassey as Contractor, and a work force of no fewer than 20,000 men, work was pushed on with great vigour; meanwhile the Nithsdale interests working from a spearhead at the northern end, in the shape of the Glasgow, Paisley, Kilmarnock & Ayr Railway, sponsored a line that from its very inception was a deadly rival to the Caledonian, namely the Glasgow & South Western. It obtained access to Carlisle over the metals of its 'enemy', by running powers over the last 8½ miles from Gretna Junction. The G&SWR was opened in 1850 and, although it might have been set down as a parallel route and as such an unnecessary proliferation, time was to show that there was plenty of traffic for both it and the Caledonian. Thus by 1850 there were three main lines northward from the Scottish Border.

Communication with Ireland involved rather different considerations. That country was in a state of great social disturbance and distress, and relations with England were such as to inflame politics at very short notice. The daily conveyance of the Irish mail between London and Dublin was a matter of the highest priority and with the introduction of railways, the question of the route to be followed became a matter of some urgency. The mail coaches had taken the Holyhead road, the present A5 highway, transferring their load to the Admiralty sailing packets at Holyhead harbour; but construction of a railway to Holyhead would involve crossing the Menai Strait.

In any case, after the construction of the London & Birmingham, the Grand Junction and the Liverpool & Manchester railways conveyance of the Irish mail was transferred from Holyhead to Liverpool. By this change in route, the time from London to Dublin had been reduced from 32 to 22½ hours in 1839. Great though this improvement was, however, the sea passage was relatively long and ideas were not long in coming for railway routes through North Wales that would reduce the sea passage to a minimum. Having in mind the major constructional task in crossing the Menai Strait, Brunel and the Great Western Railway worked out a scheme for a shorter direct route across Wales to a harbour on the Lledr peninsula, from which the distance to Kingstown would be no more than five or six miles greater than that from Holyhead.

Brunel proposed going in an almost direct line from Worcester through Ludlow to Montgomery, then after a short spell in the Severn Valley the line was to be taken in the most grandiose Brunellian style under the flanks of Cader Idris and so to Dolgelley. The climax, so far as scenery was concerned, would have been a magnificent coastal run round the head of Cardigan Bay and across the Lledr peninsula to the lonely little bay of Porth Dinllaenn, or, as it is now rendered on maps, Port Dinlleyn. At the time there was nothing there except a tiny fishing haven, but Brunel would have turned it into a major packet station. The influence of the Post Office and the Admiralty strongly favoured Holyhead, however, and so came the Chester & Holyhead Railway with Robert Stephenson as engineer. Except in the crossing of the Conway estuary and the Menai Strait, it was a relatively easy line to construct, running on coastal flats, with occasional tunnelling through headlands as at Llysfaen and Penmaenbach. There was a short, spectacular piece of work at Penmaenmawr where, after skirting the base of the mountain of that name, the line was carried on a viaduct actually in the sea. The building of the great tubular bridge across the Menai Strait was one of Robert Stephenson's greatest achievements but it was not finished by the time the Post Office required the Irish mail service to be routed via Holyhead. The Irish Mail, the first train in Britain to have an official name, was inaugurated on 1 August, 1848. Since the bridge was not completed, mails and passengers were conveyed across the Strait by coach over Telford's suspension bridge and put on to another train at Llanfair. The Britannia tubular bridge was opened in 1850.

The completion of the Chester & Holyhead Railway was the final link in the building up of what came to be recognised as Britain's premier main line railway, the London & North Western. That company was formed in 1846 by the amalgamation of the London & Birmingham, the Grand Junction, and the Manchester & Birmingham. This last named was a relatively small concern which extended no further south than Crewe. But the amalgamation also brought the pioneer main line railway into this combine, because the Liverpool & Manchester had been absorbed by the Grand Junction in 1845. It was this heritage that led to the claim of the London & North Western to be the oldest established firm in the railway business, to the annoyance of the east coast rivals, who eventually took the Stockton & Darlington into their fold. The North Western, however, evidently considered the existence of the Stockton & Darlington before 1830 as a mere north country colliery track, and not a real railway! The North Western also came to include the Lancaster & Carlisle, the Manchester & Leeds, and the Chester & Holyhead. The connection of lines longitudinally was a form of amalgamation favoured by Parliament. What was opposed, to the extent of outright refusal of authority, was the amalgamation of parallel or duplicating lines. This, it was considered, would destroy competition and set up monopolies.

A cross-country link of great importance, projected originally under the name of the Sheffield, Ashton-under-Lyne, & Manchester, was built amid the growing uncertainties and vicissitudes of the pre-Mania days. C. B. Vignoles was appointed as Engineer, a young man with a dashing and exuberant personality, who was apt to be carried away with his own enthusiasm. The outstanding feature of the line was to be the great tunnel under Woodhead Moor, by far the longest yet to be attempted in England. Kilsby, on the London & Birmingham, which caused Robert Stephenson so much trouble was 2425yd long and the notorious Box on the Great Western was 3230yd; yet Woodhead, blasted through the millstone grit of the Pennines, was to be 5300yd long. Vignoles greatly underestimated the cost, but even so frightened the shareholders to such an extent that the initial cost, or rather the original estimate, was reduced by making the bore only large enough to take a single track. Furthermore no allowance was made in the estimates for any accommodation for the workmen. In wild upland country there were no towns or villages where the huge body of navvies could be lodged. But it was neither his faulty estimates nor his lack of provision for the workforce that caused the downfall of Vignoles. He became carried away in the fever of the first wave of the railway mania and allowed himself to become deeply involved in share dealings. This would have been bad enough but he involved a number of his personal friends and when things went wrong, there was a financial catastrophe that compelled his resignation and incurred heavy loss to himself and his friends.

The board of the company called in Joseph Locke and after taking the measure of the job, he told them that the tunnel would cost *twice* the £98,000 estimated by Vignoles. That was in 1839 and such were the appalling difficulties encountered in driving that single-line bore that it took six years to complete, with a casualty list of 28 killed, 200 seriously injured or disabled, and 450 lesser accidents. The irony of it all was that the single line bore was very soon found to be inadequate and in 1847 the railway began the boring of a second single-line tunnel, parallel to the first, and this took another five years to build. The Manchester, Sheffield & Lincolnshire Railway, as the line became, quickly grew into a major west-east artery and eventually a strongly competitive route for the Manchester-London passenger business.

CHAPTER 3

Growing Pains

The Mania, disturbing as it was, and ultimately distressing to so many simple souls who lost all their savings, was not the greatest among the upheavals that fomented the early growth of main line railways in Great Britain. While financiers and speculators, many of very questionable integrity, stirred the passion for new railway promotion almost to the point of frenzy, the established managers, their engineers and operating officers became locked in a struggle of such national importance that a Royal Commission was set up to try and resolve the acute differences of technical opinion that had developed. The supreme catalyst in what became known as the Battle of the Gauges was I. K. Brunel, Engineer-in-Chief of the Great Western. Many years before this railway was projected, George Stephenson had been consulted about the gauges of various new and quite isolated enterprises following his initial involvement with the Stockton & Darlington. His reply to each was always the same: 'Make them all the same. They may be a long way away from each other now, but they'll all be joined up one day'.

Brunel thought otherwise. He dismissed the 4ft 8½in gauge as quite unworthy of the great enterprise to which he had been appointed engineer. While he was far too much of a realist not to appreciate the great inconvenience and delay that would occur at interchange stations where his broad gauge of 7ft met the 4ft 8½in, one can be fairly sure that he confidently expected that the success of the broad gauge would turn the scale. Once it was established and in operation its advantages would be so overwhelmingly apparent that all other railways would have their gauges altered to agree. In this, of course, he

Above: A very early view of Charing Cross station, South Eastern Railway, showing the first signals, and 2–4–0 locomotives. *(Courtesy Westinghouse Brake & Signal Co Ltd)*
Below: On the GWR in broad gauge days: one of the Gooch 4–2–2s *Dragon* at Didcot. *(British Railways)*

Above: London & North Western Railway up express on Bushey troughs, hauled by Webb three-cylinder compound No 2058 *Medusa* of the Dreadnought class. *(L&GRP Collection)*
Below: Great Northern Railway, one of the final batch of 8ft singles No 1003 on a down train near Hadley Wood. *(The late C. Laundy)*

made a grave misjudgment of human nature. Instead of being impressed by the grandeur and potentialities of the broad gauge, the Stephensons, Locke and their associates just 'dug in', as it were, and their managers backed them to the hilt. There was a very marked feature running through all the evidence given before the Gauge Commissioners, between 6 August and 18 December 1845. While the opponents of the broad gauge, who in sheer numbers virtually swamped those who supported it, generally based their arguments upon the far greater mileage already constructed on the narrow gauge, and the inconvenience of interchange at places where both gauges existed, the broad gauge supporters, and above all Daniel Gooch, dwelt upon the technical advantages and its greater possibilities for future development.

But one after another the protagonists of the narrow gauge were so confident that they could, with their smaller equipment, do anything that the broad gauge could do that the Commissioners could well be gathering a bank of mixed feelings. In addition to this the broad gauge lobby minimised the inconvenience of the break of gauge of which its opponents made so much. What clinched the argument in favour of the narrow gauge more than anything else, however, was the evidence of General Sir J. Willoughby Gordon, Quartermaster-General of the British Army. He inveighed heavily against the delay and inconvenience there would be when moving troops and their equipment if a break of gauge were to be involved in the course of an urgent troop movement. The possibility of war with France and an attempted invasion of Britain was talked about freely and the QMG's worries in this respect carried considerable weight. It was not that one gauge was superior to the other; it was the simple fact that there was a far greater mileage of narrow than of broad gauge. As a result of this long hearing, the Gauge Commissioners would like to have seen a definite veto placed upon any further construction on the broad gauge, but in drawing up legislation that eventuated as the Gauge Act, Parliament rather watered down the recommendations of the Commission, to permit further broad gauge extensions and branch lines of the Great Western Railway and its associated lines.

During the evidence taken by the Commissioners it became more widely known that at one time there had been a *third* gauge in England, 5ft. When the Eastern Counties Railway obtained its Act of Incorporation in 1836, with John Braithwaite as Engineer, a number of directors of the new company were anxious to use Brunel's 7ft gauge, but Braithwaite considered it an unnecessary expense and reported against it. He favoured 4ft 8½in, but as it was then assumed that the Eastern Counties would be as much a loner in East Anglia as the Great Western and its allies hoped to be in the West Country, he was asked to make an independent recommendation. Braithwaite told the Commissioners:

> I arrived at that 5 feet gauge in this way: I found that the locomotive engine was defective in several particulars; one, as to its generative power, the space we had for boiler room; next, as to the number of wearing parts; I thought that each of them ought to have, if we could afford it, a little more room, allowing a little more wearing surface, but more particularly with regard to the boiler. The tubular system then being very much adopted, it struck me that if we had a little more space between the tubes we should have a more quiet action of the water in the boiler, and consequently, less ebullition, and therefore with a diagram and section of my engine, I added to all its different bearings, and I added what I considered sufficient additional space to the tubes, the sum of which gave me 4 feet 11¾, and upon that I assumed that 5 feet would be about the thing.

His suggestion caused something of a sensation, particularly among those directors who were also on the boards of the London & Birmingham, and of the Grand Junction. But after a great argument his suggestion won the day, the voting being 20 for and only 2 against. So the Eastern Counties was actually laid down on the 5ft gauge. It did not remain so for long, however, and Braithwaite told the Commissioners in another long and highly verbose statement why the gauge was changed to 4ft 8½in. The arguments for having 5ft instead of 4ft 8½in studied today seem quite unconvincing, and one can sense that the Commissioners thought so too! At one time Vignoles had been associated with Braithwaite in the surveys for the Eastern Counties Railway. He was then very much the stormy petrel of the railway engineering world and had strongly advocated a 6ft gauge — characteristically different from everyone else! But he dropped out of the Eastern Counties picture at an early date. In retrospect Braithwaite's choice of 5ft gauge seems all the more extraordinary in that the neighbouring Northern & Eastern from Shoreditch to Cambridge had adopted 4ft 8½in. One can only suppose that his advocacy before the ECR board was of the same length and verbosity as his speeches before the Gauge Commissioners!

It was mentioned in the preceding chapter how the Northern & Eastern was considered as a likely springboard for a new direct line to the north. It had aroused instant opposition from the established companies and in March 1844 the *Railway Times* declared that it was its duty to 'protest against, and denounce this newest of reckless speculations and all concerned in its concoction'. Hudson steamed into the attack with great vigour and promoted lines from the Midlands cutting clean athwart its proposed route, with lines from Swinton via Doncaster and Gainsborough to Lincoln, and from Nottingham via Newark, to join the first named, also at Lincoln. Despite Hudson, however, by the end of April of that same year there were no fewer than *four* distinct proposals for new north to south trunk lines between York and London. All or whichever was actually to be built, would be in competition with the existing route from Euston, via Derby.

Such was the volume of support gathering for a new line that Hudson and the London & Birmingham management felt that while they could not prevent the eventual emergence of a new competitor the best policy was to engineer a series of offensive and defensive alliances, and the construction of new links and branch lines to strangle any new trunk line at its birth. So, in addition to the cross-country lines to Lincoln it was proposed to extend the Cambridge line to link up with a Midland branch to Peterborough and also, by the deviation of the authorised Peterborough extension of the Eastern Counties, to build a line to the north via March, Boston, Lincoln and Doncaster. Hudson, as a director of the Eastern Counties as well as the Midland and of the companies centered upon York, was in a strong position to engineer the entire project and what the *Railway Times* termed a 'great and valuable alliance' was expected, as that newspaper put it, 'to spread peace in the railway kingdom from Yarmouth to Holyhead'. What a hope! The *Railway Times* had not yet assessed the calibre of the men who were sponsoring the one project, out of the four aiming to build new north to south trunk lines, that was coming to the fore as a definite scheme, the London & York. The one dissident factor in the 'great and valuable alliance' against it was that, as mentioned in the previous chapter, it was a time when the London & Birmingham and the Grand Junction were not on the best of terms; so when the London & York invited Joseph Locke to be its engineer he readily accepted.

By the early summer of 1844 Parliament was becoming so alarmed at the prospect of being swamped with railway bills in the next session as the Mania worked up to its height, that it was felt necessary to give preliminary examination to bills before they actually came before a full session of Parliament so a committee of five under the chairmanship of the President of the Board of Trade was set up in August. It is of interest to recall that W. E. Gladstone had just been succeeded in this latter office by the Marquis of Dalhousie who later, as Governor General of India, played such a big part in the early planning of railways in the sub-continent. The first railway proposal to be examined by the 'Five Kings', as the Board of Trade committee was duly nicknamed, was the London & York, and the tremendous fight it had to get through all the subsequent Parliamentary procedures took nearly two years. It eventually received the Royal Assent on 26 June 1846 and the London & York then became the Great Northern Railway Company. The original main line ran via Hatfield, Huntingdon and Peterborough and then over the Lincolnshire loop line through Boston, Lincoln and Gainsborough. The main line north of Peterborough through Grantham, Newark, and Retford was not opened until 1852.

Locke did little towards the Great Northern, except make some preliminary surveys, because very soon after his appointment the strained relations between the Grand Junction and the London & Birmingham were sorted out and he felt he could not serve a new line which would so obviously be a rival to his older associates. He was succeeded by William Cubitt, who built the splendid line that has been an epitome of fast running ever since. Of course Hudson, by protocols straight and devious, flamboyant and insulting rhetoric, strove might and main to block it at every stage in the Parliamentary procedure—and afterwards; but his reign as Railway King was soon to crash in flames as spectacularly as the chariot of Phaeton. As long as things appeared to be flourishing all was well, but when at the end of 1848 the bursting of the Mania bubble sent the shares of even the soundest concerns tumbling, questions began to be asked and a single point raised in February 1849 at the half-yearly meeting of the York, Newcastle & Berwick Company brought about his ruin. It was then revealed that by wholesale juggling of the capital and revenue accounts of two northern companies of which he was Chairman, the York & North Midland, and the York, Newcastle & Berwick, the shareholders of both had been presented with an entirely false picture and the dividends paid were far higher than were justified.

He had a way of appropriating surplus shares, distributing some to friends and taking the rest as his personal property; perhaps the most astonishing instance was his acquisition of no fewer than 10,894 Newcastle & Berwick shares, but signing for them on behalf of the company. Revelations like this, of a man who had enjoyed the confidence of investors, had a catastrophic effect on the railway share market and brought about his own downfall. It was sad to think that a man who did so much to build up the English main line railway network, whom no lesser person than Gladstone once described as 'a man of great discernment, possessing a great deal of courage and rich enterprise, a very bold and not at all an unwise projector' should have fallen so low. Today, railway history remembers his great, rather than his shady achievements and it is a measure of that esteem that in his own native city of York one large building in the complex of the Eastern Region head-quarters is named Hudson House.

Turning now from the north to the south of England, there is the interesting case of the Brighton railway. This was not a project of financiers, investors, or even of business men; it was the brain child of a professional civil engineer, Sir John Rennie. Employing C. B. Vignoles on the survey he put forward a plan for The Surrey, Sussex, Hants, Wilts & Somerset Railway Company. It did nothing but provoke opposition schemes, until by 1836 there were six different routes from London to Brighton for Parliament to consider. Shorn of all its western tentacles, Rennie's line was the one eventually authorised, but it was not until 1841 that the railway was opened throughout. Even then the Brighton Railway did not run on its own metals for the entire way from London Bridge. It began over the London & Greenwich — the first railway in London — then it passed on to the London & Croydon until reaching a station with the euphonious name of Jolly Sailor — now the more prosaic Norwood Junction. Then there were actually six miles of its own line, to Coulsdon, after which it passed on to the South Eastern Railway until reaching Redhill. The Brighton line originally abounded in picturesque names. The junction with the SER near Coulsdon was Stoats Nest, and Redhill — actually Redstone Hill — was at first Reigate Junction. At the Brighton end there was a signal box named Lovers Walk, the name surviving for some sidings.

The South Eastern Railway, for all its potential as a great trunk line to the Channel ports, had a most curious beginning. It was authorised as early in railway history as 1836 but was manoeuvred into a strangely ineffective position. While Dover, as a veritable railhead of all England so far as overseas travel was concerned, was an obvious goal, there was little local trade to be gathered there and the line had to depend to a large extent upon intermediate traffic. Even so the route chosen looks a bit odd. The natural one would surely have been that of the historic Dover Road, crossing the Medway at Rochester, and continuing through Faversham and Canterbury. But the original plan took the line through Croydon, then on a hilly course through the North Downs via Oxted, and then from Edenbridge running straight through Tonbridge to Ashford and thence to the coast at Folkestone. Then, when the Brighton Railway was projected, Parliament, noting the roughly parallel courses of the Brighton and South Eastern lines south of Croydon, suggested they should use the same tracks as far south as Redhill. Thus the South Eastern became saddled with a very roundabout route in its exit from London, and the inconvenience of sharing part of it with another company.

At its eastern end the South Eastern Railway came to possess one of the major lions of British railway topography and engineering, first the huge viaduct across the Foord Gap at Folkestone, and then the line beneath the chalk cliffs with its succession of famous tunnels, great cuttings and embankments. The line was completed through to Dover in 1844 and with good management it soon began to earn steady if not spectacular dividends. In the mid-1850s, when many early railways were experiencing great difficulties because of the slump following the bursting of the mania bubble, the South Eastern showed every sign of a solid, secure business that had shown enterprise and skill in building up its system. It was strongly entrenched in South-East London, had a main line and excellent system of feeder branches in Kent, and was building up a flourishing cross-Channel business at Folkestone, while holding the mail contract at Dover. But then, in 1858, a single-tracked local line, called the East Kent, was opened between Strood and Faversham. No railway nurtured in the wildest days of the mania had a less stable financial basis; yet by simply outrageous management audacity, this ramshackle concern grew so fast that in 1861 it snatched the Continental Mail contract from under the very noses of the South Eastern!

In 1858 the SER had an opportunity to secure control of the East Kent, but the proposal was turned down and the infant railway obtained its Act to extend westward to St Mary Cray. With all thoughts of amalgamation thrown to the winds the East Kent, in 1859, changed its name to London, Chatham & Dover. There was no disguising the intentions of its management, but how this chronically insolvent concern managed to find the cash to build its extensions into London and from Faversham through Canterbury to Dover is a much longer story than can be told here. Equally there was the capture of the mail contract. The plain fact remains, though, that the line was completed through from London to Dover in time for the continental service to begin in July 1862. Audacity apart, however, the Chatham, as it became known, had become head over ears in debt in the process of its rapid expansion and in 1866 it went bankrupt. Nevertheless traffic was kept moving and although the luckless investors went through a long, grim, and apparently unending privation, so far as the railway network of Great Britain was concerned, another main line had been added to the map. Furthermore, although at the beginning of the railway era many sagacious men felt that there was no need for more than a single main line down the backbone of Kent, when the activities of the two one-time cat-and-dog rivals came to be properly co-ordinated, the existence of both was on many occasions to prove a godsend in the handling of continental traffic, quite apart from the purely local facilities each provided.

Further west, the adverse report of the Gauge Commissioners did not, at first, damp the ardour of the Great Western. No embargo had been placed upon the projection of extensions to the broad gauge system, but while the field was relatively clear in South Wales, strong opposition developed in the South West, from the London & South Western, and in attempted advances to the north from the London & North Western. Down in the West Country the Great Western, on Brunel's recommendation, was sponsoring a new direct line to the west, avoiding the long detour through Bath and Bristol. It became known as the Exeter Great Western, and would have served Frome, Yeovil, Crewkerne and Honiton. In 1845 the country was still completely clear of railways between the London & Southampton and the Bristol & Exeter, but strangely enough, although the Southampton interests were threatened, as such a line would have blocked their hoped-for westward advance from Basingstoke through Salisbury, the strongest objection came from Bristol & Exeter. That line had not then become part of the Great Western and its management saw in the development of the direct line to the west a threat to their traffic. Had the Exeter Great Western project gone ahead, however, undoubtedly on the broad gauge, it would have sealed off the west of England beyond the Wilts, Somerset & Weymouth line running south from Trowbridge through Westbury, Frome and Yeovil.

Intransigence within the broad gauge club not only robbed the Great Western of a line that would have been of immense value later, but also laid the country west of Salisbury wide open for the extension of the London & South Western. The splendid express route that was built later and of which Joseph Locke was engineer, took the LSWR to Salisbury by 1857 and to Exeter by 1860. Locke was Member of Parliament for Honiton, but he died before the line was in operation, at the early age of 55. In the Mania days there had been many schemes for railways in north-west Devon and Cornwall, but they had lapsed. The arrival of the LSWR at Exeter revived some of these and a new rivalry sprang up between a number of narrow gauge projects and the longitudinal extension of the broad gauge, via the South Devon and the Cornwall Railways. There is no doubt that the South Western had its eyes on the West Cornwall Railway, which ran from Truro to Penzance, and which was *narrow* gauge. It should be noted that in this period of railway history the term 'narrow gauge' usually referred to 4ft 8½ in gauge, today known as standard gauge, and not to the smaller gauges now embraced in the description narrow gauge. If the South Western, working through the untapped territories of North Cornwall could get to Truro, and link up with the West Cornwall the westward advance of the broad gauge could be halted. The break of gauge at Truro was causing friction between the Cornwall and the West Cornwall companies, and while the former had the right to demand the conversion of the West Cornwall to broad gauge, the South Western felt that if it could get to Truro before the demand became an actual threat it could prevent it altogether. Unfortunately for the South Western, the finance necessary to build the lines through North Cornwall was not forthcoming.

The Great Western collision with North Western interests came from the advance of the broad gauge from Oxford to Birmingham and Wolverhampton. This would perhaps not have raised so much antagonism in itself had not the project contained a branch line from Fenny Compton to Rugby. To see the broad gauge arriving in such a stronghold of narrow gauge interests would have been too much. By way of appeasement the Great Western was required to lay in mixed gauge between Oxford and Birmingham, but the branch line to Rugby was eventually omitted.

CHAPTER 4

The Scottish Network

By 1850 three major trunk routes were established northward from the Border. Those of the Caledonian and North British were closely allied with the west coast and east coast routes from London, but the Glasgow & South Western at first had to pick up what traffic it could from the three English lines feeding into Carlisle, from Lancaster, Maryport, and Newcastle. Little more than a decade passed, however, before yet another main line from the north came into Carlisle. The North British, embarking upon a period of unbridled expansion, first projected a long branch line from Edinburgh to Hawick and followed this with the Border Union Railway, which carried the line from Hawick over Whitrope summit and down into Liddesdale. What began as lengthy branch lines became a potentially important trunk route, though at its opening through to Carlisle in 1862 it was not yet a serious rival to the older Scottish companies working into the city. But the seeds of fierce competition were there and the Caledonian was faced with rivals on both sides, the Glasgow & South Western for Glasgow traffic, and the North British for that to Edinburgh. As if this were not enough, in 1854 the Border Counties Railway was projected to build a line from Hexham, on the Newcastle & Carlisle, to join the Border Union line at Riccarton Junction and thus be in a position to tap traffic from Tyneside, without the necessity of going through Carlisle.

The build-up of the North British was rapid and far-reaching. It absorbed, as from 1865, the Edinburgh & Glasgow, the most level railway in Scotland. It was begun in 1838 and built to compete with a well-established canal business; its gradients seemed to have been laid out in the style of a canal! The engineering works were tremendous, but neither the original owners nor the North British exploited this magnificent road to provide a really fast service between Glasgow and Edinburgh. It was indeed not until the diesel age in railway traction that full advantage was taken of its remarkable alignment and level track. The acquisition of the Edinburgh & Glasgow by the North British gave the company an excellent and independent access to the west coast, but things were not so easy north of Edinburgh. The great inlets of the Firths of Forth and Tay presented natural obstacles to the establishment of speedy railway communication up the east coast of Scotland and, although the North British became very busy absorbing local lines in Fife, the company was not yet in a position to help its English allies in competing for the Anglo-Scottish traffic north of Edinburgh. The great estuaries had to be crossed by ferry and overall progress by the Edinburgh & Northern or, as it later became, the Edinburgh, Perth & Dundee was very slow.

Meanwhile the consolidation of the Caledonian line to Aberdeen was progressing rapidly. When the chain of railways from Carlisle to Aberdeen was first completed a through journey over this 240 miles included 11 different sections and nine separate companies. The Caledonian itself ran from the south to Garriongill Junction; then, in progressing to Castlecary, the lines of three companies were traversed, namely the Wishaw & Coltness, the Monkland & Kirkintilloch and another short stretch of Caledonian ownership, before joining the metals of the Scottish Central at Castlecary. This continued the journey to Perth. Following this came passage over six small railways which were eventually amalgamated to form the Scottish North Eastern. By 1866, however, the entire chain except for one small and inconvenient intrusion had been amalgamated into the Caledonian. The exception was 52 chains, 0.65 miles, of the Monkland & Kirkintilloch Railway, between Gartsherrie and Garnqueen South Junction. The anomaly arose, however, because in 1865 the Monkland &

Kirkintilloch had been absorbed by the North British. This alien ownership remained for no less than 83 years. In 1923 the Caledonian and the North British passed into the LMS and LNER groups respectively so it was not until nationalisation in 1948 that the whole line from Carlisle to Aberdeen came under one ownership. In the heat of the 1895 race, which is referred to in some detail in Chapter Six, one could imagine there would have been strong temptation to block the Caledonian train by adverse signals on this section. The risk of this was minimised because, although the signal boxes at each end were provided and equipped by the North British, the Caledonian appointed, paid, and clothed the signalmen concerned. This was a reasonable arrangement because there were no North British passenger and very few goods trains using the line, while from the Caledonian viewpoint it formed part of the West Coast Royal Mail route from London to Aberdeen.

The build-up of the G&SWR in the south-west corner of Scotland was a colourful business, in keeping with the adventurous way in which the train service was operated in later years. Stranraer was the focal point of activities in the south-west but it was not the primary objective in the earliest railway promotion in the area. What GSW men called 'the long road', from Kilmarnock down to Carlisle, was opened throughout in October 1850. There then developed a great project with the high sounding name of the British & Irish Grand Junction Railway. Already Government packets crossed the North Channel between Portpatrick and Donaghadee, but the railway that was eventually projected as the Portpatrick obtained its Act in August 1857 to build a line from Castle Douglas to Portpatrick, with branches to harbours at both Stranraer and Portpatrick. The GSW had opened a branch line between Dumfries and Castle Douglas in November 1859, but the Portpatrick & Wigtownshire, as the name under which the Portpatrick Railway eventually took shape, was worked at first by the Caledonian. This may have seemed rather strange, but the latter company had a subsidiary from Lockerbie to

Dumfries, known as the Dumfries, Lochmaben & Lockerby Junction, opened in 1863, and had running powers over the line from there to Castle Douglas. The Portpatrick line was opened as far as Stranraer in March 1861 and to Stranraer Harbour and to Portpatrick in 1862.

Meanwhile the line from the north was slowly working its way through the very hilly country south of Ayr. It was built up as a series of separate enterprises, but unlike certain other routes that came to have considerable importance for through traffic, the various constitutents seem to have been consistently short of money. There was first the Ayr & Maybole Railway, 9 miles long, opened in October 1856. Then came the Maybole & Girvan, another 13 miles, opened in May 1860. Then there was a long pause and it was not until October 1877 that the 31 very heavily graded miles of the Girvan & Portpatrick Junction Railway, which joined the Portpatrick line at Challoch Junction, was brought into service. This line traversed some of the wildest and most desolate country in the south-west of Scotland, and had some appropriately fearsome gradients: 1 in 54 from Girvan itself up to Pinmore Tunnel; a bank seven miles long mostly inclined at 1 in 67 from Pinwherry southwards and a deadly 1 in 57, northbound from New Luce, with the dreaded 'swan's neck' S-curve in the middle of it, in a lonely, quite unpopulated moorland waste. The Girvan & Portpatrick Junction had running powers from Challoch Junction over the last 6½ miles of the Portpatrick Railway proper. But the Girvan line was in financial trouble very soon and in 1881 a court injunction was issued against it, prohibiting the use of the line westwards from Challoch Junction, pending payment of large outstanding arrears in the agreed running powers payments. The Glasgow & South Western came partly to the rescue in helping the Girvan company to run a service as far south as New Luce, the last passenger station before Challoch Junction, where there was no station. It is not altogether surprising that a remunerative service did not quickly materialise in this desolate countryside. Nor was the Portpatrick & Wigtownshire itself entirely out of trouble, despite the working arrangement with the Caledonian, and in 1885 it was reconstituted into a joint railway, with the parent companies being the Caledonian, Glasgow & South Western, London & North Western, and Midland. The two large English companies had considerable interest in fostering traffic over this line to Ireland, via Stranraer, though the actual working of the line was the responsibility of the two Scottish companies.

In dealing with railway development geographically, it is perhaps inevitable that there are times when the story gets out of strict chronological order and reference to Midland participation in the Portpatrick & Wigtownshire line has anticipated by nine years the arrival of the Midland, in its own right, at Carlisle. However, this chapter is concerned with purely Scottish developments and reference to the two lines to Stranraer is necessary to fill in the picture of main line network operated by the Glasgow & South Western. We must now go back more than thirty years to the construction of main line railways in the Highlands.

The point of great distinction about the railways in the Highlands of Scotland is that their inception in the first place was due entirely to social and local interests. They began in the ancient burgh of Inverness. The prospects of lucrative business was virtually nil. No company promoter of the mania type and no tycoon of the London stock market would have given it a thought. It was the burghers of Inverness and the chieftains of some of the great clans who determined they must have better communication with the outside world, and they were fortunate in having in a fellow townsman a civil engineer of great distinction in Joseph Mitchell. The one cloud on the horizon was Aberdeen, certain citizens of which thought they would like to have a railway to Inverness. The two towns were hereditary foes. The Invernessians had not the slightest intention of making their outlet to the south through Aberdeen even though it could well have been the cheapest way to link up there with the Scottish North Eastern. But Aberdeen got in first and in 1845 the Bill for a Great North of Scotland Railway was presented to Parliament, to build a line from Aberdeen to Inverness. This was in March of that year and no more than a month later the prospectus of the Inverness & Perth Railway was issued. The latter, with Joseph Mitchell as engineer, and Locke and his partner J. E. Errington as consultants, proposed a line eastwards along the shores of the Moray Firth through Nairn to Forres, striking out to meet and hopefully block the advance of the Great North of Scotland towards Inverness, and then south to pass at high altitude through the heart of the Grampian mountains and so down towards Strathtay.

Aberdeen interests strove by might and main to obstruct the passage of the Inverness & Perth Bill. The opposition briefed their learned counsel to dissect and ridicule Mitchell's proposals to cross the Grampians at an altitude of nearly 1500ft in the Pass of Druimuachdar and at first they succeeded. In the 1846 session of Parliament the GNSR line was authorised, from Aberdeen to Huntly, but the Inverness & Perth Bill was thrown out. Although the people of Inverness were naturally very disappointed at this rebuff, it was soon apparent that the GNSR was in no position to take up the powers granted to it by Parliament. Its promoters were revealed as a pretty incompetent lot, with no substance to back the vigour and loquacity with which they had promoted their own project and decried that of the Inverness & Perth. In 1846, the mania in England was working up to its height. The Board of Trade, guided by Lord Dalhousie's 'five Kings', was examining every railway project with great care and the burghers of Inverness and the Highland chieftains, who associated so closely with them, made their next step rather more cannily. In 1853 they presented to Parliament a Bill for a railway from Inverness to Nairn. It was authorised in the following year and unlike the GNSR they got to work at once. The cutting of the first turf on 21 September 1854 was made a

Above: London, Brighton & South Coast Railway: the first all-Pullman express to Brighton, at Tooting Common, hauled by one of the first Billinton 4-4-0s, No 202 *Trevithick* of the B2 class, nicknamed 'Grasshoppers'. *(L&GRP Collection)*

Below: South Eastern & Chatham Railway: Continental boat express emerging from Shakespeare's Cliff Tunnel near Dover, hauled by D class 4-4-0 No 730. *(L&GRP Collection)*

Above: Early days on the London extension of the Great Central: the 5.40pm Marylebone–Manchester express passing West Hampstead, hauled by Pollitt 4–2–2 No 967. *(L&GRP Collection)*

Below: A fascinating period piece on the Midland at Elstree: a heavily loaded down express hauled by a 4–2–2 'Spinner' approaching, while an equally immaculate 0–6–0 goods engine is shunting in the yard. *(L&GRP Collection)*

gala occasion, which a large proportion of the population of Inverness turned out to witness. The next step was the promotion of the Inverness & Aberdeen Junction Railway, to continue the line from Nairn eastwards through Forres and Elgin to Keith, where it was expected to meet the GNSR. This section was opened in 1858 and by then the Inverness party were ready to re-launch their cherished project of a direct line to the south, using Forres as the starting point.

The Inverness & Perth Junction Railway Company was formed in 1860 and was a corporate effort of the Highland people as a whole. The landed proprietors took the lead, but all classes subscribed their quota. Contributions ranged from a princely £335,000 from the Duke of Sutherland down to the humble one-share mite of the poor, but nevertheless public spirited crofters. There was once again a good deal of opposition from the Aberdeen interests but, in view of the ineptitude of the GNSR management and its already shocking record of operation, these arguments counted for little and the Bill went smoothly through to receive the Royal Assent in July 1861. The worthlessness of the opposition to the line over the Grampians, on so-styled technical grounds, was shown by the speed and efficiency with which the line was built. The new railway was fortunate in its engineer, Mitchell. He had to build across sedgy moorland, past rugged granite outcrops, and beside the courses of mountain rivers that could change from a trickle to a raging torrent in a matter of hours. Another very important feature of the line was the care taken not to disfigure the landscape. The great landowners had been very generous in their support and in surveying the route Mitchell took particular care to align it to avoid destroying their forests, or intruding more than necessary upon the prospects enjoyed from their homes. It is remarkable that in such a terrain, with all the difficulties of transport for materials and the vagaries of Highland weather that the 104 miles between Forres and Dunkeld authorised by the Act were completed and open for traffic in less than two years from the cutting of the first turf.

The Perth & Dunkeld Railway, which began from a junction with the Scottish North Eastern (afterwards part of the Caledonian) at Stanley, had been opened in 1856. It was amalgamated with the Inverness & Perth Junction Railway in June 1863. Two years later this line amalgamated with the Inverness & Aberdeen Junction, and from June 1865 the combine took the title of The Highland Railway.

The extension of the line to the Far North was accomplished by the incorporation of several separate companies in succession, all of which were eventually absorbed into the Highland Railway. The various stages are shown in the following table:

FAR NORTH LINES

Company	Extent	Distance (miles)	Year incorporated	Year opened
Inverness & Ross-shire	Inverness to Invergordon	31½	1860	1862
Ross-shire Railway Extension	Invergordon to Bonar Bridge	26¼	1863	1864
Sutherland Railway	Bonar Bridge to Brora*	32½	1865	1868*
Duke of Sutherland's Railway	Golspie to Helmsdale	17	1870	1871
Sutherland & Caithness	Helmsdale to Wick; branch to Thurso	86½	1871	1874

*Line built only to Golspie (26½ miles). No more money available!

One of the most interesting and picturesque of Highland lines is the Dingwall & Skye, authorised in June 1865 to make a railway from Dingwall to the Kyle of Lochalsh. The original Act provided for construction of a pier at Strome Ferry, on Loch Carron, but in view of the heavy cost of construction it was agreed, in 1868, that the line should be completed only as far as Attadale, at the head of this sea-loch, and that a pier should be built there for the steamer service to Skye. Actually this decision was reversed in the following year and the line was completed to Strome Ferry in August 1870. This remained the terminus of the line for 27 years, when the extension to Kyle of Lochalsh, authorised in 1893, was completed.

Transferring attention now from the West Highlands to the east coast, the North British, in its anxiety to secure a monopoly of the business in Fife and as much of it in Angus as it could wrest from the Caledonian, had built up an extraordinary tangle of loops and branches, perpetually hamstrung by having no definite main line from north to south, and having to depend for through communication on ferries across the estuaries of the Forth and the Tay. These inevitably gave an uncertainty to the working, especially at times of stormy weather, and the North British acquired the reputation of being one of the most unpunctual railways in the kingdom. With its intricate programme of connections with English railways south of Edinburgh this was unfortunate. The first step towards improving the situation was the decision to build a great bridge across the Firth of Tay, from Dundee. The North British was unfortunate in its choice of Thomas Bouch, as engineer. At the time he was a man of soaring reputation but actually much of his work, when analysed critically, was faulty in basic principles. Added to that, he paid little attention to detail and none whatever to supervision of the work of his contractors. In fact the first Tay Bridge, both in design and execution, was a disgrace to British engineering and the marvel was not that it collapsed but that it stood up as long as it did. It passed the Board of Trade inspection in May 1878; in June 1879 Queen Victoria passed over it on her way from Balmoral and knighted Bouch, and in December of that same year it fell, taking a train with it and all its passengers and crew to their deaths. The second and present Tay Bridge, a very massive structure of undistinguished appearance, designed by W. H. Barlow, was opened for traffic in 1887.

Before the collapse of the first Tay Bridge, Bouch had been commissioned to design the bridge needed to cross the Firth of Forth and he was proposing a gigantic suspension bridge, with towers 600ft high. Naturally enough, the disaster to the Tay

Bridge ruined his reputation and the company had to reconsider the entire project. From the outset the undertaking was so vast that a separate company had been incorporated, originally in 1873, but reconstituted in 1882. It was, of course, of vital interest to other railways beside the North British and of the ten directors of the Forth Bridge Company, two each were appointed by the Great Northern, North British, North Eastern, and Midland railways, and only two independent members. The Midland was actually the largest guarantor, with a 32½ per cent liability. The Great Northern and the North Eastern share was 18¾ per cent each, leaving 30 per cent for the North British. In spite of all that has happened since in the construction world, the Forth Bridge, designed by Sir John Fowler and Sir Benjamin Baker, is still one of the most famous engineering structures in the world and, despite its colossal size, so superbly proportioned as to be one of the most beautiful. It was opened by King Edward VII, when Prince of Wales, in March 1890.

The Forth Bridge was the last link in the build-up of the principal main line network of Scotland, save for the Carr Bridge direct line of the Highland, authorised in 1884, but not completed until 1897. Nevertheless, two long lines, never very profitable but extremely popular with railway enthusiasts and to a limited extent with summer tourists, must be noticed. Neither could be classed as a main line in the same sense as that of the Caledonian between Carlisle and Glasgow or that of the North British from Edinburgh northward over the Forth and Tay Bridges, but both tapped remote districts, largely inaccessible at a time when the road network in the Highlands of Scotland was so hazardous as to be almost negligible. The two lines are, of course, the Callander & Oban and the West Highland. Both were built to open up the country with few prospects of remunerative traffic and attractive dividends. The former was sponsored and eventually worked by the Caledonian, and the latter by the North British. The history of both is long and complicated enough to furnish material for entire books, referred to in the bibliography. Here it is only necessary to add the dates of their completion to provide notable sections of the overall map of Scottish railways. The Callander & Oban was opened throughout in June 1880, the West Highland to Fort William in August 1894 and the Mallaig extension in 1901.

CHAPTER 5

Proliferation — Heightening the Competition

The Midland Railway, with Hudson at the helm, had expanded and profited greatly in the period of the Mania; but the revelations of his devious tactics in the direction of some of the northern companies so tarnished his reputation that he resigned from his chairmanship of the Midland in 1849. Notice of his resignation was contained in a letter to John Ellis, who succeeded him. It was couched in somewhat evasive terms, as reported in F. S. Williams's *History of the Midland Railway* thus: 'It stated that, during his chairmanship of the Midland Company he had been identified with the York, Newcastle & Berwick Companies, all of which hitherto had had a common interest; but now that the Great Northern Railway had been sanctioned, and new relations were arising, and new alliances were contemplated, he thought it would be more satisfactory to the shareholders of the Midland Company that he should resign the office. Mr Ellis added that this was also a resignation by Mr Hudson of his position on the direction'.

It was a very neat and diplomatic way out. It was obvious that the Great Northern would become closely associated with the two companies based on York in developing an East Coast service from King's Cross to Scotland, which would be an embarrassment to the Midland, and that if he had stayed with the latter he might have been accused of having a foot in each camp; but as he had, in fact, withdrawn in disgrace from his associations with the York & North Midland, and with the York, Newcastle & Berwick, it would not have seemed to matter either way. As events turned out, the completion of the Great Northern in 1850, albeit only as yet via the Lincolnshire loop line, had a far more serious effect upon the fortunes of the

Midland than in providing an excuse for Hudson to slide out without facing the shareholders. The opening of the Great Exhibition in London in 1851 brought bumper traffic to the Great Northern and to the London & North Western, but a disappointing and most serious decline to the Midland. Their traditional outlets towards London was effectively by-passed by the Great Northern and holiday traffic in other directions dried up. Ellis told the shareholders: 'The fact is there has been nobody going to Cheltenham; scarcely anyone going to Scarborough; and the little Matlock line has experienced a decline in its receipts this year amounting to 20 per cent. All this is entirely owing to the Exhibition'.

From being in a key situation in the East Midlands and the North East, the Midland now found itself in a constrained position and with the very poor results for 1851 before them, the board felt it was essential that they should be permanently identified with some railway having a line to, and a terminus in, London. It is indeed remarkable to recall that negotiations were opened for a complete amalgamation of the Midland with the London & North Western and when these hung fire Derby actually turned to the Great Northern in the hopes of effecting a similar arrangement. The latter company also treated this advance with some restraint. Then at a special meeting of Midland shareholders at Derby in November 1852, a proposal to effect complete amalgamation with the LNWR was carried by a very large majority and a Bill in accordance with that decision was submitted to Parliament. This, however, was not the kind of amalgamation then favoured, but in view of the magnitude of the finance involved and the likelihood that it could be the forerunner of several similar proposals from railway companies feeling the effects of competition, a select committee of the House of Commons was appointed. This advised the House not to allow any amalgamation during the current session of Parliament and reported strongly against any other large amalgamations that would set up monopolies.

The Midland was therefore left on its own between its old and new neighbours on each side. At the height of the Mania, however, in 1847, an Act had been passed for construction of a line from Leicester southwards to Hitchin. It had originally been projected to embarrass the progress of the London & York, with the idea of cutting across its tracks and making contact with Hudson's interests in East Anglia. In the event, however, no attempt was made to build the line, and in July 1850 the powers conferred by the Act expired. In view of the disappointment over the amalgamation proposals and continued loss of passenger traffic to the Great Northern, powers for again taking up the lapsed authority were made and progress was made to the completion of the line at Hitchin in May 1858. This provided for running powers over the Great Northern from Hitchin to King's Cross. So Midland trains, hauled by Midland engines were at last running into London. It was soon found, however, that the conditions were highly unfavourable. By the terms of the arrangement, the Great Northern was required to provide accommodation for both goods and passenger traffic, but it would have been contrary to human nature if it had not given preference to its own business, however profitable the tolls extracted from the Midland might be.

The Midland had in the heart of its original territory one of the richest coalfields in Great Britain, that of South Yorkshire, and as early as the 1850s there was an enormous volume of traffic to the south. The opening of the Erewash Valley line north to Clay Cross had provided an admirable route for through coal trains to the south, avoiding Derby, but the difficulty for the Midland was to get rid of the traffic it had so effectively collected further north. The original route had been over the Midland Counties southwards to Rugby, where trains were handed over to the London & North Western. The latter company was already feeling the strain even though it had laid down a third line, purely for up trains, between Bletchley and London. There were times, though, when the

LNW was so choked as to be unable to accept any more coal trains from the Midland and messages were sent, stopping all trains for certain areas around London which were blocked solid. On one occasion the Midland had a queue of coal trains five miles long waiting to get into Rugby. Some of this traffic was in due course switched to the Great Northern, with equally frustrating results. The Midland was in the unhappy position of seeing its passenger business dwindling still further, of paying heavy tolls to both the Great Northern and the London & North Western, and reaping a sour-apple harvest in the form of endless complaints from its customers in London because of the non-arrival, or chronic delays to the supplies of coal they had ordered.

It seemed as though the Midland was now condemned to be second best. Although in possession of great riches on its original territory it was dependent upon others to get them to the markets. Naturally the Midland went to the Great Northern and more or less demanded better facilities; the reply was that the GNR was quite prepared to double its line — at the expense of the Midland! This would have meant not only widening the earthworks, rebuilding many of the overbridges, doubling the width of the great Digswell Viaduct at Welwyn, and doubling no fewer than *nine* tunnels, but the building of an entirely new terminus for the Midland in London. And having done all that, it would have been delighted to charge tolls for the use of the new line. There was another danger in this proposal too. The country between Bedford and London, lying between the territory of the Great Northern and of the London & North Western was then devoid of any railways, save small branches laterally from one or other of the trunk lines, and the Midland feared that it might easily be taken up with yet another rival. So it was no more than natural when the Midland decided the time had come to spend money, not in financing the widening of the Great Northern but in building a line of its own into London over which, of course, no tolls would be payable for its use. So the line southwards from

Bedford was promoted, going through Luton and St Albans, and entering London through Haverstock Hill and Kentish town. It proved much more expensive than originally estimated, because with astonishing foresight it was decided at the last minute to make it wide enough from the outset to take four tracks. This was a decision that paid off handsomely in years to come.

Before the line from Bedford into London was completed another new Midland line had been brought into operation, namely that from Ambergate to Manchester, through the magnificently rugged scenery of the Peak District. There were some heavy engineering works on this line, notably Dove Holes Tunnel, and several large viaducts; but this line, opened in 1863, put the Midland into direct competition not only with the North Western, but with the combined strength of the Great Northern and the Manchester, Sheffield & Lincolnshire for the London-Manchester traffic. The Great Northern and the MS&L operated a highly competitive service via Retford, MS&L (later the Great Central) engines working as far south as Grantham. But although the Midland, through the opening of its new line over Peak Forest, became a competitor for the London-Manchester traffic, in which the North Western held most of the trump cards from its easy route and lesser mileage, the Midland went into partnership with the Great Northern and the MS&L in setting up a *third* competitive route between Manchester and Liverpool, that of the Cheshire Lines Committee. Hitherto the LNWR using the original Liverpool & Manchester Railway via Rainhill and over Chat Moss more or less had the field to itself; although the Lancashire & Yorkshire Railway also had a line, it was at first rather a roundabout route and so badly operated as not to put up any serious competition. The resurgence of the Lancashire & Yorkshire, or rather its upsurgence was to come later, and to put both the LNWR and the Cheshire Lines very much on their mettle.

In 1864 another short but very important section of the

Midland Railway was approved. By that time the rising eminence of Sheffield as a great manufacturing centre demanded better railway connections. Hitherto it had been served by a branch of the Midland from Rotherham and it was very roundabout and inconvenient from the viewpoint of service from the south. The only direct service from London was by the Great Northern, to Retford, and thence over the MS&L. The new Midland proposal was to build a line branching off the North Midland at a point just one mile north of Chesterfield and then take a steeply graded route through Unstone, with a long tunnel at Bradway to reach Dore, and approach Sheffield down a thickly wooded valley. This would place Sheffield on a through route to the north and enable a strongly competitive service to be built up. At one time however many of the most important trains did not use the Sheffield loop line, but made instead long non-stop runs down the course of the North Midland. Nevertheless by its construction the Midland had established direct connection between Sheffield and Derby, Nottingham and Leicester, of which it held a monopoly until the very end of the nineteenth century, when the Manchester, Sheffield & Lincolnshire decided upon its supreme gamble of the London Extension, and changed its name to Great Central. Until then the MS&L did not extend even as far south as Nottingham.

One of the most important developments in the second half of the nineteenth century in Northern England was the upsurge of the Lancashire & Yorkshire Railway, from being a ramshackle sprawling local concern into one of the really great railways of Britain. It was strange that the company had been a very profitable concern for its shareholders who, in 1872, received no less than 8¾ per cent on ordinary shares. But its public image, in its operating slackness and chaotic time-keeping, was deplorable. Plans were drawn up for a full amalgamation with the London & North Western. It would have seemed that the management was anxious to be rid of responsibility, before the equipment fell into a still further state of disrepair. The LNWR for its part, would have been glad to eliminate a potential competitor and that remarkable dividend was an attraction to the shareholders of the larger company. But Parliament threw out the amalgamation Bill, on the grounds that it would create a monopoly, and the LYR was left to go it alone. One of the most important improvements subsequently undertaken was the construction of two cut-off lines to provide a more direct route, completed in 1889, between Liverpool and Manchester, instead of the existing meandering line that went through Wigan and Bolton. The first town was by-passed by the Pemberton loop and a new direct line, 13 miles long and quadruple-tracked, was built from Windsor Bridge Junction, 1.8 miles out of Manchester, to Crow Nest Junction, where it trailed into the old line from Bolton to Wigan. These two new lines shortened the distance between Manchester and Liverpool to 36 miles and in due course the LYR was able to compete with the LNWR in providing a service between the two cities in 40 minutes. Very heavy capital expenditure was involved and, although the all-round smartening up throughout the line was much appreciated by the travelling public, the shareholders suffered and by 1885 the dividend had dropped to 3¼ per cent. In the process however the LYR was developing into a first class railway.

The expansionist tactics of the Midland take a very prominent place in the history of British railway development from 1870 onwards. It was not only in its outlets to the south that its management felt it had put up with a position that was definitely second best, but it also wanted a share in the increasingly important Anglo-Scottish traffic. Across the Border the Glasgow & South Western was in a similar position of having to put up with second best. It had no outlet of its own at Carlisle and the North Western had effectively blocked an earlier attempt of the Midland to penetrate further north, by building a branch line southwards from Low Gill to make a head-on confrontation with the Midland's Little North

Western line at Ingleton. The year was 1866 and the obstructionist tactics at Ingleton and further north towards Midland traffic led the Midland management to consider building a line of its own to Carlisle. There seemed to be two ready-made lines of outlet for its business into Scotland, over the North British and the Glasgow & South Western, both of which were apparently in competition with the Caledonian. But when the Midland came to explore the situation in more depth it found to its dismay that the G&SW and the Caledonian had obtained Parliamentary sanction for an alliance that was little short of full amalgamation. If then the Midland went ahead with its proposed independent line to Carlisle it would do no more than feed into the empire of its direst enemies, the west coast companies. The Midland therefore had to do everything it possibly could to prevent the implementation of the arrangements already authorised between the G&SWR and the Caledonian. In this of course the Midland had the strong support of the North British.

At the outset, however, the Midland was once again in a position of second best: in getting to Carlisle at all it was dependent on the North Western via Ingleton and Low Gill. The Midland therefore determined to make a line of its own to Carlisle and to combine with this project an amalgamation with the Glasgow & South Western. This of course aroused great opposition from all the established interests at Carlisle. The North Western in particular, appreciating that if the Midland built its own line to Carlisle it would stand to lose a considerable sum in tolls, offered much more attractive terms, so much so that the Midland, faced with the high capital cost of a new direct line, placed a Bill for abandonment. This aroused objections in a way that was not expected. The North British and the Lancashire & Yorkshire railways had both welcomed the Settle & Carlisle project of the Midland because it would enable them to inaugurate Anglo-Scottish services independently of the North Western. They opposed the abandonment Bill with such vigour that Parliament, always ready to quash anything that looked like a monopoly, threw it out. The Midland was therefore left with the responsibility of building 73 miles of railway through some of the most difficult country in England. Although financing this project would strain the resources of the Midland to the utmost, when it was finished it would provide a vital connecting link between four systems, the North British and the Glasgow & South Western in Scotland, the Midland and the Lancashire & Yorkshire in England.

Having been finally saddled with the job, the Midland spared neither pains nor money in building a line that was worthy of this virtually unique position. It would have been understandable in the circumstances if the easiest way round had been taken to lessen constructional costs, if deviations had been made to avoid awkward geographical locations, if the line had been carried over the mountain ridges, as Locke had taken the Lancaster & Carlisle at Shap Summit. The Settle & Carlisle, on the contrary, was built as a fast express route, with not a single speed restriction below 75 to 80mph throughout its length. If there was a deep valley athwart the direct line it was spanned by an immense viaduct; if there was a mountain ahead it was passed in a long tunnel. The only way to deal with rocky eminences was to blast clean through. The result was one of the grandest pieces of railway in the British Isles, amid scenery of sublime mountain grandeur. By its opening to express traffic in 1876 the Midland, in partnership with the Glasgow & South Western on the one hand and with the North British on the other, became a major competitor for Anglo-Scottish traffic, and by its association with the Lancashire & Yorkshire and with its own line to the South West from Birmingham to Bristol, an important new series of through carriage services to Scotland were inaugurated. It was the potential of business over the Settle & Carlisle line that led the Midland to invest so substantially in the Forth Bridge Company, referred to in the previous chapter, which led eventually to the running of through services from the Midland line to Aberdeen, Perth, and Inverness, all across the Forth Bridge. At one time the Bristol sections of the night expresses to Edinburgh and Glasgow were heavy enough to form a train of their own.

Midland competition to south-west England was severely threatened from December 1886 by the completion of the Severn Tunnel. This not only shortened the main line from London to South Wales but made available to the Great Western and London & North Western railways in partnership a new and highly competitive route from the North East to the South West; the GWR and LNWR not only ran services from Liverpool and Manchester to Bristol, via Shrewsbury, Hereford, and the Severn Tunnel, but included connections, via Stalybridge and Huddersfield from Leeds and Bradford. The forthcoming final conversion of the gauge on the Great Western main line to the West of England opened the way for further through train services from the north and these soon came to include facilities from the Midland and the North Western routes north of Bristol. The Midland indeed features prominently in many of the train service developments in the latter years of the nineteenth century, and references must be made to two joint lines which, originating in local and unpropitious circumstances, became parts of main lines that carried very heavy passenger traffic in the summer holiday season. These were the Somerset & Dorset and the Midland & Great Northern Joint Lines.

How the broad gauge Somerset Central, 12 miles long, from Highbridge to Glastonbury, opened in 1854, and the narrow gauge Dorset Central, 10¼ miles long, from Wimborne to Blandford, begun in 1856, grew by various extensions to link up and eventually form a through line from Bath to Bournemouth is a longer story than can be told here in any detail. But it is interesting to recall that the original affiliations of the first two sections were to the broad gauge Bristol & Exeter and to the narrow gauge London & South Western respectively. The last mentioned remained so to the very end, but at its northern end the Somerset & Dorset Joint Railway as it eventually became cast off all its associations with the broad gauge and teamed up with the Midland at Bath. The joint ownership was between the Midland and the London & South Western, begun in 1876 when there were through carriages to Bournemouth from Bradford, Leeds, Newcastle-on-Tyne, Sheffield and York. It was never a high speed route, primarily because of the very severe gradients between Bath and Evercreech Junction, but it was fascinating to the railway enthusiast.

The second joint line in which the Midland was concerned was no less so. Again it was a hilly road that carried immense passenger traffic in the holiday season. The Midland & Great Northern, with its picturesque orange-yellow engines, collected traffic from the Midlands and conveyed it through Spalding and King's Lynn to Melton Constable where the main line forked in three directions, to Cromer, Yarmouth and Norwich. There was another feeder line from Peterborough through Wisbech. The Act, vesting in the Midland and Great Northern railways responsibility for taking over the former Eastern & Midlands Railway, was dated June 1893. Its build-up had been long and complicated, but it took its place as an important holiday route and today one can rejoice that a portion of it, between Sheringham and Weybourne, is preserved and in working order, though operated by ex-GER locomotives.

Above: Great Northern Railway of Ireland: a southbound train entering Balmoral station, hauled by 4–4–0 locomotive No 72 *Daffodil. (L&GRP Collection)*
Below: Great Southern & Western Railway: a view from above of Glanmire station, Cork, with an express for Dublin ready to leave. *(L&GRP Collection)*

Above: L&NWR: the up day Irish Mail near Colwyn Bay, hauled by a Precursor Class 4–4–0 in pre-first world war days. *(Locomotive Publishing Co)*

Below: GNR: the 2.20pm Scottish express near Potters Bar hauled by non-superheated 4–4–2 No 1440. *(The late C. Laundy)*

CHAPTER 6

An Outburst of Speeding

During the latter part of the nineteenth century the Midland Railway was the catalyst in many competitive actions. Faced with the position of being second best it forced its way to an independent entry to London. It blasted a way through the limestone of the Peak to create a third route to Manchester. Faced again with the prospect of remaining second best, it built a magnificent route of its own to Carlisle. All this, however, was not enough for its great General Manager, James Allport. He was determined to fight his competitors by more subtle means. In 1872, at his recommendation, accommodation for third class passengers was provided on all trains, where hitherto the principal expresses had carried first and second class only. Then, as if this were not enough, it was announced that as from 1 January 1875, second class would be abolished and what had previously been the comfort of second class travel was conferred on holders of third class tickets at the statutory third class fare of one penny per mile. Great were the prophets of woe who, on the one hand deplored what the French call the democratisation of travel, and on the other expected the early bankruptcy of the Midland Railway. In fact neither catastrophe eventuated and it was not long before other railways began to follow the example of admitting third class passengers to all trains, if not yet going to the extent of abolishing second class.

It was the discrimination in classes carried on certain trains that led, in the summer of 1888, to the most exciting event that had taken place on the railways of Britain since the Rainhill locomotive trials of 1829. Until 1887 the East Coast companies — Great Northern, North Eastern and North British — had

71

been carrying first and second class passengers only on their Special Scotch Express, which left King's Cross at 10am each morning. It had preferential treatment in the way of speed and covered the 393 miles from London to Edinburgh in nine hours, including all stops, one of which was the luncheon interval at York. For some little time the corresponding West Coast train which left Euston also at 10am had been carrying all three classes and took ten hours from London to Edinburgh. The Chairman of the LNWR, the austere Richard Moon, was much against any form of speeding up, not because he disliked speed as such but because it increased the costs of operation, in coal consumption and in maintenance charges on track and rolling stock. He held firmly to the view that an end-to-end average speed of 40mph was high enough for any express train and accepted with much reluctance an acceleration forced upon them when the Post Office demanded an average speed of 42mph for the Irish Mails between Euston and Holyhead.

Then in November 1887 the East Coast companies decided to provide third class accommodation on the 10am Special Scotch Express which meant that for the basic fare of one penny per mile a passenger could get to Edinburgh a full hour quicker if he took the train from King's Cross rather than from Euston. At first the West Coast companies were inclined to ignore this obvious challenge. The Midland, despite the possession of its magnificent Settle & Carlisle line, was not able to run on equality with either East or West Coast route, because of its greater mileage and the physical difficulties of the North British line north of Carlisle. Instead it concentrated on providing what was unquestionably the most luxurious accommodation of the three, both for first and third class. By the end of 1887, however, the West Coast route was definitely experiencing a marked decline in third class bookings from London to Edinburgh. So was the Midland. But the managements of the North Western and the Caledonian had a long and difficult way to go before they could convince Richard

Moon that an acceleration was essential, and he exercised such a tight control on matters of policy that he *had* to be convinced, before they could go ahead. During the spring of 1888, the East Coast companies had been expecting some acceleration from their rivals, but when it did come the suddenness of the announcement and the magnitude of the cut in time took the East Coast alliance completely by surprise. Only at the very last minute did the North Western reveal that on June 2 the Day Scotch Express, as the 10am departure from Euston was then called, would be quickened by a full hour to both Edinburgh and Glasgow. The surprise was so complete that no response came from the East Coast companies for a full month.

It is interesting to compare the booked point to point speeds on which the rival trains operated during the month of June 1888. The North Western still retained its stop to take up passengers at Willesden Junction, allowing 9min for the initial run of 5.4 miles from Euston, and a restart at 10.11am.

WEST COAST ROUTE

Section	Distance Miles	Time min	Av Speed mph
Willesden-Rugby	77.2	91	50.9
Rugby-Crewe	75.5	88	51.5
Crewe-Preston	51.0	60	51.0
Preston-Carlisle	90.1	113	47.7
Carlisle-Edinburgh	100.6	133*	—

*Including stop to divide train at Carstairs.

EAST COAST ROUTE

Section	Distance Miles	Time min	Av Speed mph
King's Cross-Grantham	105.5	129	49.0
Grantham-York	82.7	100	49.6
York-Newcastle	80.6	102	47.3
Newcastle-Berwick	66.9	86	46.6
Berwick-Edinburgh	57.5	77	44.7

The East Coast group had seven miles less to run and only four stops against six, so that they could maintain the overall time of nine hours with easier intermediate running. Furthermore the luncheon interval at York was of 30min duration, whereas the West Coast, even before the acceleration, had not allowed more than 25min at Preston.

The calendar of acceleration for these two expresses thereafter read as follows:

DATE	ROUTE	TIME: London to Edinburgh
July 1	East Coast	8½ hours
August 1	West Coast	8½ hours
August 1	East Coast	8 hours
August 6 +	West Coast	8 hours
August 13	East Coast	7¾ hours
August 13	West Coast	7 hr 38 min
August 31	East Coast	7 hr 27 min

*Schedule not previously announced
+ Bank Holiday Monday!
°Fastest actual overall times

It was an astonishing development with the two fastest runs giving overall average running speeds of 56.2mph by the West Coast and 57.7mph by the East Coast. The number of intermediate stops had then been reduced to three on each route: Crewe, Preston and Carlisle on the one hand, and Grantham, York and Newcastle. Both routes, risking damage to the passengers' digestions, had cut the luncheon stops to 20 minutes! By August 13 however both sides evidently felt that things had gone far enough and at an East-West conference on August 14 it was agreed that the times of 7¾ hours by the East Coast and eight hours by the West should remain for the rest of the summer and that an extra half-hour should be added to each schedule for the winter of 1888-9. Even so, the improvement in service over that provided during the previous winter was striking enough, involving cuts in overall time from London to Edinburgh of ¾ hour by East Coast and no less than 1½ hours by West Coast. It must be emphasised that this all arose from one of the two rival groups giving better travel facilities to *third* class passengers. Glasgow had, of course, come off second best in the West Coast accelerations. The Edinburgh section of the 10am from Euston, from August 6 onwards, ran as a separate racing train, starting off with a non-stop run to Crewe. The second section, principally for Glasgow, made the usual intermediate stops and, as one commentator sarcastically observed, collected the passengers who had been left behind by the racing first portion!

In September 1888 the *Pall Mall Gazette*, then very well informed on railway matters, carried a long article summarising the results and effects of the 1888 Race to the North, as it became known. But the comments of that newspaper were not confined only to the achievements of the racing 10am trains. It included this striking paragraph:

A foreigner taken on to the midnight platform at Shap in the earlier nights of August would have been surprised to see *five* expresses roaring through within two hours, one laden with 'Horses and Carriages only', another full of beds and lucky people whose rest the North Western will not allow to be broken by the entry of a single passenger between Euston and Perth, all five steaming without a stop the ninety miles from Preston to Carlisle, except one (from Liverpool and Manchester) which takes the 105 from Wigan in a breath. Down the adjacent Eden valley he might almost have heard the *three* Midland night expresses, two sweeping without a stop from Skipton to Carlisle, one in a longer burst of ninety-six miles from Keighley. Away on the East Coast *five* Great Northern trains would be doing similar deeds, two from York to Newcastle (80 miles) without a stop, all five from Newcastle to Berwick (66 miles), and two of them without a pause from Newcastle to Edinburgh, 124 miles. Still more incredulous would our visitor have been when told that these were not *luxe* or 'limited' trains with extra fancy fares, but that all alike conveyed the common third class traveller. [But not in sleeping cars it should have added.]

In referring to the night trains the newspaper scented the prospects of an even more severe speed contest. In what direction? The cast was put dramatically:

The main cause confronts us when we see those three stupendous towers of steel which loom above the horizon of Edinburgh. When the Forth Bridge is finished the North Western and Caledonian will have to struggle hard if they to retain much of the traffic to Dundee or Aberdeen, and may possibly be robbed of some of that to Inverness.

The approaching completion of the Forth Bridge was to have a profound effect upon the railway network of Scotland and, so far as the East and West Coast routes from London were concerned, one had only to study the mileages to appreciate how the West Coast supremacy to Perth, Aberdeen and Inverness was threatened by this gigantic development. The distances from the respective London termini, after opening of the Forth Bridge became:

SCOTTISH STATION	DISTANCE East Coast	MILES West Coast
Perth	440.9	449.9
Dundee	451.9	471.0
Aberdeen	523.2	539.7
Inverness	584.8*	593.8*

*Via Highland Railway, original line

In 1890 the Inverness Direct Line via Carr Bridge, although authorised and under construction, was not yet open. The alternative route to Inverness for the East Coast, via the Great North of Scotland line to Keith and Highland thereafter, was 46.6 miles longer than via Perth, even before the Carr Bridge line was opened. After the completion of the Forth Bridge in

March 1890, the night service to Perth in the holiday season of that year by the East Coast and Midland routes was:

King's Cross	dep.	7.45 pm	8 pm	—
St Pancras	dep.	—	—	7.50 pm
Edinburgh	dep.	4.35 am	4.55 am	5.23 am
Perth	arr.	5.50 am	6.15 am	6.45 am

The fastest East Coast train made an average speed of 43.8mph, but one can see from the foregoing comparison the extent to which the Midland was handicapped towards any speed contest by its longer route and physical disadvantages, despite its enterprise in every other direction. At first, however, after the adjustments to the East Coast timetables after the completion of the Forth Bridge there were no outward signs of any renewal of the rivalry of 1888. The East Coast had an advantage of 16½ miles in the total distance from London to Aberdeen, and with 15 minutes difference in the running times from London, the spirit of the truce agreed in August 1888 was preserved, but in 1891 a source of rivalry began to brew up in Aberdeen. Each year the presence of the Court at Balmoral was making travel to Deeside increasingly fashionable and the GNSR had a train that left Aberdeen at 7.50am—one of those stupidly characteristic timetable arrangements of the old Great North that failed to connect with important trains from the south. The West Coast 8pm from Euston did not arrive in Aberdeen until 8.5am and although the corresponding East Coast train was booked in at 7.45am, it was usually so late that it missed the connection anyhow. The last thing to enter the heads of the GNSR at that time would have been to keep the Deeside train waiting for 'fashionable' passengers from London!

For the summer service of 1893 the West Coast companies, planning an acceleration of their train to reach Aberdeen at 7.50am persuaded the Great North to make its departure at 8am. There was good business in this, because the Caledonian was almost invariably punctual and the connection would be a reality. The East Coast also made their arrival 7.35am preserving the traditional 15 minutes difference, but the North British had not then attained the reputation for punctuality that it afterwards achieved, and operation in the old Waverley station in Edinburgh continued to be chaotic at times of traffic pressure. Furthermore, despite the outward display of friendship between the East and West Coast groups, in Scotland, the Caledonian and North British were on cat and dog terms and watched each other like two rival Highland clans of old. The Caledonian, indeed, devised a most ingenious method of blocking North British trains where the routes converged at Kinnaber Junction, north of Montrose. The North British was made to pay heavily, and not only in cash, for having the right of running powers from Kinnaber Junction to Aberdeen. The North British discovery of the delightfully simple ruse by which the Caledonian was able to block the East Coast train three nights out of four, and an attempt to pull a fast one over the North British over connections at Perth, only served to sow the seeds of suspicion, distrust and rivalry that were growing up between the Caledonian and North British in the years immediately following the opening of the Forth Bridge.

It was in the early summer of 1895 that the West Coast companies took the first step towards further acceleration of the night service from Euston to Aberdeen. Finding that a connecting time of no more than 15 minutes from their arrival to the departure of the Deeside train was uncomfortably short for passengers with the mountains of luggage that then accompanied so many wealthy families on holiday, and the uncompromising attitude of the Great North in refusing to delay its departure, the West Coast partners brought their arrival time forward to 7.40am, only 5 minutes behind the East Coast, as from 1 June. The result was increased friction at Kinnaber, and a month later the East Coast cut a quarter of an hour off their journey time. There then followed a month of time cutting without precedent as the two sides strove to outbid the other by apparently legitimate means, of timetable announcements, but in the case of the West Coast running well ahead of their advertised times. For example, as from 15 July, with no more than 12 hours prior warning, the West Coast brought their published arrival time to 7am and then proceeded to run as much ahead of it as they could. They had in fact a target time of 6.35am and actually reached Aberdeen at 6.47am on the first day. It was some little time before the East Coast companies came to realise that their rivals were sending the racing train away from intermediate stations as soon as it was ready, and not waiting for the advertised time of departure, leaving a second section of the train to pick up the passengers who were left behind; as from 29 July the East Coast accelerated the 8pm from King's Cross to reach Aberdeen at 6.25am—10 minutes ahead of the target, or working time of arrival of the Euston train, still announced as 7am.

Despite this, however, for the next three weeks the West Coast still had very much the best of it. The lines were then at their busiest, with tourist traffic building up for the opening of the grouse shooting season on 12 August. Nevertheless, the records of running during that period are amazing enough on reflection, seeing that until 15 July the arrival times had been around 7.30am.

8pm EXPRESSES	LONDON TO ABERDEEN Times of Arrival		
Date	West Coast Time	East Coast Time	Mins late
	am	am	
July 29	6.05	6.23	2 early
,, 30	5.59	6.40	15
,, 31	6.16	6.50	25
August 1	6.16	6.54	29
,, 2	6.15	6.33	8
,, 4	6.09	7.05	40
,, 5	6.08	6.25	Right Time
,, 6	6.18	6.42	17
,, 7	6.15	6.28	3

August	8	6.17	6.50	25
,,	9	6.09	6.45	20
,,	11	6.11	6.30	5
,,	12	6.12	6.20	5 early
,,	13	6.15	6.28	3
,,	14	6.13	6.22	3 early
,,	15	6.18	6.25	Right Time
,,	16	6.10	6.27	2
,,	18	6.23	6.17	8 early

The West Coast on their best runs were averaging 54mph from end to end, a remarkable achievement, and while no timetable changes were advertised during this period, a great amount of activity was going on behind the scenes. Spies were out from both sides, eavesdropping, and it was by these tactics that the East Coast became convinced that their rivals were disregarding the published timetables. Even so, in planning a very big acceleration for August 19 there was still the lingerings of orthodoxy, at any rate in Scotland, and although a definite schedule was planned on the basis of what each of the three companies felt was the best they could do, the Great Northern and the North Eastern intended to go through as fast as they could, adopting the West Coast tactics, and their operating officers thought they had conveyed the idea to their North British colleagues. Whatever the senior management of the NBR may have appreciated, however, it had not been brought home to those in charge on the platforms at Edinburgh and Dundee in the early hours of August 20, and the train which had made record time down from King's Cross, arriving in Edinburgh 10 minutes early, in 6¾ hours from the start, was kept waiting for 8½ minutes after the fresh engine had been attached and was ready to leave. It was the same, to a lesser extent, at Dundee. There was some hard running on the final length, and when the East Coast train passed Kinnaber Junction and ran on to the Caledonian line they were 8½ minutes early by the carefully planned timetable. So far as actual running was concerned the 485½ miles from King's Cross had been covered in 527½ minutes, at a very good average speed of 55.2mph, and Aberdeen was reached 44 minutes later, 8½ minutes ahead of the planned time of 5.40am. But the West Coast had done it again and were in Aberdeen 16 minutes earlier. Even without the protracted station stops at Edinburgh and Dundee it would seem that the East Coast would still have been 4 or 5 minutes behind.

The next three nights witnessed some all-out running by both sides, the like of which has never been seen since on the railways of Britain; although very much faster running is made today by the modern diesel and electric trains, the risks that were undoubtedly taken, and the boundless spirit of combat displayed by most of the train crews concerned lifted this brief episode far above the regions of orthodox railway operation. This exciting climax to the race has been told in books and in at least one television feature. Here it is only necessary to set down the bald details of the overall times achieved, and to emphasise the phenomenal change that had come over the scene, wherein a scheduled arrival time in Aberdeen of 7.35am by East Coast and 7.50am by West Coast, prevailing to the end of May, had been cut eventually to 4.40am East Coast, and 4.32am West Coast.

Date	West Coast		East Coast	
leaving	Time of	Average	Time of	Average
London	arrival	Speed	arrival	Speed
	am	mph	am	mph
Aug 19	5.15	58.3	5.31½	56.6
Aug 20	4.58	60.2	5.11	58.8
Aug 21	4.54	60.7	4.40	62.3
Aug 22	4.32	63.3	—	—

It is not really surprising that, after the incidents of the respective journeys had been fully documented and duly digested, managements felt that the speeding had gone far enough. It was on the East Coast route that most of the more hair-raising episodes seem to have occurred. It is certain that no such speeds have since been run on the East Coast route north of Edinburgh, even in this era of Inter-City 125 sets. On the West Coast the alarming derailment of the very train that had been involved in the 1895 racing, at Preston, a year later came as a shock to public opinion, and caused some of the wiseacres to say, 'I told you so'. But actually it was a case of inexperienced drivers, rather than the taking of calculated risks by highly skilled and experienced men. It was nevertheless enough to put the brake on future acceleration; indeed it ushered in a period of retrenchment and slowing down so far as the Anglo-Scottish services were concerned. The Race to the North as it had become known had shown the potentialities of the locomotives, to the extent they had been developed to that date, and that much faster train times could have become a practical proposition if the travel market had been ready for it, but as will be told in the succeeding chapter the process of evolution on the main line railways took a different turn.

By way of criticism of what was achieved in 1895, it is sometimes emphasised that the high average speeds were made with very light trains. So they were in relation to the general level of train loading, even at that time. But reviewing the fastest runs in the light of subsequent history, it is clear that in respect of train to engine weight the great runs of 1895 showed almost exactly the same ratios. This chapter may be concluded by setting some of these runs side by side, so far as this ratio is concerned.

FAMOUS BRITISH RUNS

Year	Rail-way	Route	Engine No	Name	Average Speed (mph)	Ratio Train to engine wt
1895	GNR	Grantham-York	775	(Stirling) 4-2-2	65.3	2.98
1895	NER	Newcastle-Edinburgh	1620	(4-4-0 Class M)	66.1	2.8
1895	LNWR	Crewe-Carlisle	790	*Hardwicke*	67.2	2.98
1904	GWR	Paddington-Exeter	3433	*City of Bath*	67.2	3.02
1932	GWR	Swindon-Paddington	5006	*Tregenna Castle*	81.6	2.95

1935	LNER	Newcastle-King's Cross	2750	*Papyrus*	70.8	2.81
1936	LMSR	Glasgow-Euston	6201	*Princess Elizabeth*	70.0	2.97
1937	LMSR	Crewe-Euston	6220	*Coronation*	79.8	2.96

CHAPTER 7

The Age of Pre-eminence

In the last twenty years before the outbreak of World War I, the links were forged to bring the British railway network to its zenith of route mileage, and with it to a pinnacle of elegance in style and quality of service not equalled by any other group of railways in the world. It is true that some overseas system had a few passenger trains faster than the British best, and in other aspects there were isolated features in which we were excelled; but for all round reliability, safety in operation, and frequency of service, the pioneers of the steam railway were still the leaders, as well as being by far and away the most colourful. Even into the nineties of the last century however, there were certain lines in Great Britain that went a long way towards justifying the music hall joke, and the notable reform of these wayward, albeit picturesque systems is one of the first items to be noted in this chapter. They mostly ran south of the Thames, and it is with the Brighton, the South Eastern, and the London, Chatham & Dover that I am principally concerned.

In September 1895 when the thrilling achievements of the East and West Coast routes in the Race to the North were still vividly in mind there was a long correspondence in *The Times* under the heading of 'The Crawl to the South' in which the misdemeanors of the Brighton and South Eastern railways were highlighted. Some extraordinary examples of inept management and working were quoted, and the growing volume of evidence in this correspondence inspired *The Times* to a leading article that aptly expresses the depths of ignominy into which these two railways had fallen. It is all the more remarkable because of the heights of idolatry to which the locomotive practice of the Brighton had been elevated by the enthusiasts of the day, in acknowledgement of the fascination exercised by the yellow engines of William Stroudley. Locomotive enthusiasts apart, however, this is what *The Times* had to say, editorially, on 14 September 1895:

> The Southern managers have no doubt been aware that it would be of very little use for them to attempt to rival the magnificent performances of the Great Northern and London & North Western companies. Their rolling stock and the well-established traditions of their companies put it out of the question that they should try this with success. They have hit accordingly upon another method of distinguishing themselves more suited to their capacities. They have chosen frankly a very different form of distinction, and the struggle between them now is which of them can claim to have established the slowest, the most unpunctual, and the most inconvenient service of trains. The real rivals are the South Eastern and the London Brighton & South Coast lines, and the performance of both are so singular, and their claims to the honour which they are seeking are so nearly balanced, that there are good grounds for a difference of opinion as to their respective merits. Very bad they both are, this at least the most severe critic must admit, difficult as he would find it, on a review of the evidence, to say with certainty which of the two has the better right to call itself absolutely the worst line in the country. . . .

The thick-skinned, though always excessively polite traffic departments of the two railways could withstand indefinitely the jibes of *Punch*, the ridicule of the music halls, and the remonstrances of passengers, first, second, and third class alike; but when 'The Thunderer' opened fire thus it was another matter. Something really had to be done about it. One physical feature that had provided a heaven-sent and perennial excuse for unpunctuality on both lines was the joint section of the Brighton main line between Coulsdon and

Redhill, through the long Merstham Tunnel under the North Downs. Both consistently blamed the other for late running over their entire systems or, so it seemed, upon congestion and mutual obstruction over this short length of line, and one of the first steps towards the most radical improvement of Brighton operation was the construction of an entirely new line of its own, from Stoats Nest Junction, near Coulsdon, to Earlswood. It was no more than six miles long but it had the supreme merit of by-passing Redhill and eliminating once and for all — so far as the Brighton expresses were concerned — the uncertainties and frustrations of a major junction controlled by a South Eastern signalman! There was some spectacular cutting and tunnelling work in the North Downs where the new line, on steeper gradients, climbed alongside the old and crossed in the middle of a very deep cutting before entering Quarry Tunnel; its opening to traffic on 1 April 1900 was no joke, but the beginning of an entirely new era in Brighton railway operating.

Meanwhile, the South Eastern and its arch-enemy the London Chatham & Dover had also turned over to welcome new leaves. In 1894 Sir Edward Watkin, the second 'Railway King', and a most obstinate and implacable character retired from the chairmanship of the South Eastern Railway, and with his going the way was made clearer for a rapprochement with the London Chatham & Dover. It was obviously in the best interests of the County of Kent, and of traffic to the continent of Europe that the two companies should get together, but this had been impossible while Watkin was at the head of the South Eastern. When his retirement was announced in 1894, not only from that company but from all the other lines with which he was connected, the stocks concerned sharply advanced in price on the London Stock Exchange. In 1898 the co-ordination of interests between the South Eastern and London Chatham & Dover was effected into a working union, under a South Eastern & Chatham Railways Joint Managing Committee. From that time onwards they worked as one, with engineering

Above: North Eastern Railway: the southbound Flying Scotsman hauled by three-cylinder 4–4–2 No 728. *(The late R. J. Purves)*
Below: Southern Railway: the all-Pullman Southern Belle near Purley in the late 1920s, hauled by King Arthur class 4–6–0 No 796 *Sir Dodinas le Savage. (The late C. Laundy)*

Above: LMSR: the up Royal Scot, non-stop to Euston, leaving Carlisle, hauled by Royal Scot class 4–6–0 No 6139 *Ajax*. The train includes coaches built specially for the service in 1928. *(F. R. Hebron)*

Below: LNER: the down Flying Scotsman passing through Hadley Wood, on the first non-stop run to Edinburgh in 1928, hauled by 4–6–2 locomotive No 4472 *Flying Scotsman*. *(L&GRP Collection)*

and traffic officers responsible for working as though it were now a single company. Although there was no such thing as a South Eastern & Chatham Railway Company, for the two companies remained as legal entities, anything that carried the initials SE&CR was henceforth hallmarked as a thoroughly sound and businesslike proposition. What might have been a series of duplicating and potentially redundant lines were skilfully integrated into a homogeneous network that provided an invaluable group of alternative routes for the peculiar needs of the Continental and seaside holiday traffic worked in the Kentish area as a whole.

The setting up of the South Eastern & Chatham Railways Managing Committee ushered in an age of elegance in design of locomotives and rolling stock that had previously been absent in Kent, and it happily coincided with an era on the railways of Great Britain as a whole in which the appearance and appointments of passenger coaches attained a dignity and character that had hitherto been lavished mainly upon locomotives. On the majority of lines it was not only the main line express locomotives that were so favoured; local tank and humble goods engines of all vintages were groomed and polished like so many *objets d'art*, while many of the carriages were little better than so many dog-boxes on wheels. In general only the Midland had stood apart from this criticism, because large and massive as some of the broad gauge carriages of the Great Western might have appeared, the thirds in particular were very narrow inside, with little knee room, and those occupying the centre seats would have had precious little sight of the country through which they were passing. But that was all changing in 1900. Large corridor carriages were being introduced on the Great Northern and London & North Western services, making dining cars accessible from all parts of the train instead of, as at first, confined to those taking seats in the one or two vehicles; and the exterior design of carriages was developing into handsome and distinctive styles from the utilitarian six-wheeler with an almost flat roof which had characterised British main lines during the last 30 or so years of the nineteenth century.

On some railways there was a simplification of locomotive liveries from the highly ornate displays of the nineteenth century, as in the case of the North Eastern, the Highland, and the Brighton, which latter company abandoned the greatly loved Stroudley yellow, for a more workmanlike, though little less distinctive, chocolate brown.

It was also a time in which railway publicity began to develop. The introduction of magazines devoted entirely to railways containing beautifully produced colour plates enabled the hitherto parochial ranks of railway enthusiasts, living at a time when extensive travel was the exception rather than the rule, to learn what the trains of railways a hundred miles or so from their homes looked like. At the same time the main line railways themselves began to issue attractive sets of picture postcards at what we should now consider fantastically low prices, in competition with the famous coloured cards of the then Locomotive Publishing Company, which were more expensive at one (old) penny each!

Nevertheless, in 1895 the railway network that the country was fortunate to possess in the fateful year of 1914 was still not complete. Two companies were engaged upon important developments to their systems, the first of which was the Manchester, Sheffield & Lincolnshire. In 1890 Sir Edward Watkin, the Railway King of late Victorian years, was simultaneously chairman of the MS&L, the Metropolitan, and the South Eastern, as mentioned earlier in this chapter, and it was his aim to establish a continuous line of railway under his own control from Manchester to Dover. The Metropolitan had been extending northward from London, and in 1892 it had reached Aylesbury. It was then that Watkin persuaded the board of the MS&L to project a southward extension from Annesley, nine miles north of Nottingham, to meet the Metropolitan, over 92 miles of entirely new railway, cutting through the cities of Nottingham and Leicester. The project was most bitterly opposed by all the established railway interests, particularly by the Midland and the North Western; but after a very stormy passage through Parliament the Bill received the Royal assent in 1893, though it was not until more than a year later that construction work began. The project included a stretch of entirely new line in London, from Finchley Road to a passenger terminal and goods yard at Marylebone. It was on this section, where the line was to tunnel under Lords cricket ground, that the first turf was cut in November 1894. Three years later, but still nearly two years before the line was opened to traffic, the MS&L changed its name to Great Central.

While the new railway opened for business from London, in March 1899, strenuous efforts were made to build up an indigenous traffic between London, Leicester, Nottingham, Sheffield and Manchester, in strong competition with the North Western and the Midland, but one of the most interesting facets of early Great Central enterprise was the elaborate system of through train, or through carriage, services it built up in conjunction with lines with which it was not in competition. In the north these were the Lancashire & Yorkshire and the North Eastern, and in the south the Great Western and the London & South Western. By these important associations, through carriages from the Great Central connected to Huddersfield, Halifax and Bradford; to York and Newcastle; to Bournemouth, Torquay and Plymouth, and into South Wales. Even by the early 1900s, there were very many express trains in Great Britain composed of non-corridor coaches; but not on the Great Central. It was the proud advertisement of the company that *every* express train was vestibuled throughout and had a refreshment car included. One can hardly imagine what the reaction of patrons of those early Great Central trains would have been had they been faced with the facile and all too familiar apologia of our own time: 'We regret that buffet facilities are not available on this service today'!

In the early years of the twentieth century the Great Western in its new-found standard gauge enterprise was busy eradicating its old stigma of 'Great Way Round'. The opening of the Severn Tunnel had been the first step towards one of these major cut-off projects, and the express trains between London and South Wales began running via Bath, the Bristol avoiding line, Filton, Patchway and the Tunnel. For a short time the 10am express from Cardiff to Paddington, which ran non-stop from Newport, had the longest non-stop run in the world, a distance of 143.5 miles. This particular routing was, however, no more than temporary, until what was at first called the South Wales and Bristol Direct Railway was completed. This, of course, was what we know nowadays as the Badminton line running from Wootton Bassett to a junction with the Bristol-South Wales line at Patchway. Although this was very important as an express route for London-South Wales traffic, the Great Western intended to develop its services to the south of Ireland, via New Milford, as Neyland was at first known. Indeed, in an interview given in 1897 to the editor of *The Railway Magazine*, J. L. Wilkinson, then General Manager of the GWR, said '. . . it is possible that the Paddington-Milford boat specials may be the "crack" trains of the world'. This was certainly advanced thinking, before the concept of developing Fishguard as an ocean liner port was born. Both however stemmed from the potentialities of the Badminton line, in conjunction with the Severn Tunnel. Quite apart from such prestige passenger services, the new line, opened in July 1903, proved invaluable in handling the ever-increasing coal traffic from South Wales to London, which it would have been impossible to accommodate on the route taken at first by the South Wales expresses via Bath.

A collateral major project was the improvement of the West of England main line to avoid the great way round via Bath and Bristol. This was authorised by the board of the GWR in 1895, and was in five sections, two being improvements of existing branches, and three new sections of connecting line, as follows:

Distance Miles	Section	Work Involved
19.6	Hungerford-Patney (Berks & Hants line)	Doubling existing line
14.5	Patney-Westbury	New Line
15.6	Castle Cary-Curry Rivel Junction	New Line
3.9	Curry Rivel Junction-Athelney (Durston-Yeovil branch)	Doubling existing line
3.0	Athelney-Cogload Junction	New Line

By these works, involving the construction of 33 miles of new line, the distance between Paddington and Taunton, and points west, was reduced by 20.2 miles, and with the opening of this new route throughout in 1906 it was possible to run to Exeter in three hours from Paddington (173.7 miles) and the already famous Cornish Riviera Express could be accelerated to reach Plymouth, non-stop from London in 4hr 7min.

Two further important new routes opened by the GWR in the first decade of the twentieth century concerned Birmingham. The first was highly competitive with the Midland, and in the same manner as that to the West of England consisted of a link between existing secondary lines between Tyseley and Cheltenham, the exercise of running powers over the Midland line between Standish Junction (south of Gloucester) and Yate, and construction of a new spur from the Midland at the latter point to the South Wales main line at Westerleigh Junction near Coalpit Heath. The opening of this route throughout in 1908 made possible an entirely new train service from Wolverhampton and Birmingham to the West of England via Stratford-on-Avon and Cheltenham, while via Gloucester and Chepstow there was an excellent new route from Birmingham into South Wales. It was a thorn in the side of the Midland, which already provided a service from Birmingham to the West of England by its own trains from Leeds and Bradford, via Sheffield and Derby. Furthermore in granting running powers to Great Western trains between Standish Junction and Yate an embargo was placed, for very many years, on the use of any larger passenger locomotives than 4-4-0s, through a long-held, though mistaken assessment of the effect of certain locomotive types on underline bridges.

The last Great Western cut-off line, the completion of which in 1910 brought the entire British railway main line network virtually to its final form, was an 18¼ mile stretch across virgin country between Ashendon and Aynho Junctions to complete the short route from Paddington to Banbury, Birmingham and the North. The more southerly part of this route was obtained with joint ownership with the Great Central, in a rather subtle way. The Great Western management was anxious to eliminate another great way round, to Birmingham, via Reading and Oxford, on which it was at very much of a disadvantage against the LNWR; sensing that the Great Central was somewhat uneasy in its dependence upon the Metropolitan for its entry into London, the GWR decided to play upon this, by suggesting to the GCR the advantages of having an alternative. The GWR already had a branch line from High Wycombe to Princes Risborough, and another authorised from Acton to High Wycombe. It was put to the Great Central that if it made use of these lines on a joint basis, by very little extra independent construction on their part, it would have a good alternative route into London. The purely Great Central parts would be from Grendon Junction to Ashendon and from Northolt Junction to Neasden. By this proposal the Great Western got the Great Central to pay a big share of the cost of what eventually became the shortened route to Birmingham. The final link, the Ashendon-Aynho cut-off line via Brill and Bicester, was opened for traffic in 1910, and the Great Western was thereby able to compete on level terms with the LNWR for Birmingham and Wolverhampton business.

It was a time when railways were the pre-eminent means of inland transport, not only for what is now called Inter-City business, but for everything. Local horse-drawn omnibuses connected village communities with the nearest railway station, and it was only in some of the larger cities that electric trams were beginning to take some of the traffic previously handled by suburban services of the main line railways. Also, although the previous antics of less efficient lines like the Brighton and the South Eastern had been passed off by those who did not have to use them regularly as something of a joke, there was an all-round awareness of the need to improve standards of operation. In safety, British railways had a record that was undoubtedly the best in the world, and although the 20 year period now under review included several bad accidents, in relation to density of traffic and number of passengers carried, the casualty list was very small. In efficiency and punctuality of day to day working, the London & North Western Railway stood very high, partly due to the high investment in improved junction layouts at points of heavy traffic interchange. Notable examples were the complete separation of goods and passenger lines at Crewe, the elaborate system of interconnecting junctions south of Rugby, and the intricate network of lines at Chalk Farm, where lines leading into Camden goods terminal were segregated and kept clear of the passenger lines leading towards Euston. These had only been projected at the end of the present period, but had it not been for the outbreak of war in 1914 the scheme would have been completed much earlier than was actually the case.

All through the period under review traffic was booming on all the old-established lines. The shareholders of the venturesome Great Central had a bad time of it, but on some lines, notably the Midland, the volume of freight traffic was a positive embarrassment. Coal was a staple traffic of the Midland, and its progress from the collieries feeding into the main line of the former North Midland, down the Erewash Valley and eventually on to the main line to London was at times appallingly slow. The fault was largely due to the earlier traditional methods of regulation—or rather the lack of it.

The routine passing on of trains from one signal box to the next could not cope. No one in higher authority had any clear idea where trains were. Coal trains were parked in sidings for hours at a time because signalmen were keeping the running lines clear for passenger trains, and in really bad instances such coal trains, often heavy enough to require two engines, never turned a wheel during the whole time the engine crews were on duty. This situation, which was reacting seriously upon the receipts of the company, was tackled following the appointment of Cecil W. Paget as General Superintendent; beginning from an experimental control system installed in 1907 at Masborough, near Rotherham, he evolved the practice that in principle came to form the basis of all British railway operation.

As initiated on the Midland the telephone was the basis of the whole scheme. Every morning the controller of a Division held a telephone conference with each of his district controllers so that Headquarters was acquainted with the general traffic position throughout the length and breadth of the system. Signalmen at key points were required to telephone to district control the time at which *all* trains passed their box. Passenger stations had to report the loading of the principal express trains so that divisional control could, if necessary, arrange for extra coaches to be added. A certain district control might report a glut of traffic; divisional control would then arrange for extra trains to clear it, and if the reception areas could not take it at once, intermediate accommodation had to be found, quickly. The essence of the whole scheme was to keep a constant watch on train movement on the principle that the best way to deal with congestion is never to let it occur. On the Midland it was an immense success, and after the grouping of railways in 1923, discussed in a later chapter, it was gradually applied to many other areas of the British railways. At this stage the principal means of communication must be under-lined, and was the keynote of success: it was the *telephone* — no time for sending telegrams. Instant action was needed.

CHAPTER 8

Inception and Development in Ireland

Until 1922, when by Treaty the Irish Free State was established, and only those counties of Ulster now part of Northern Ireland remained within the United Kingdom, the railways of Ireland were subject to the provisions and scrutiny of the Board of Trade in London. Before very many miles of railway had been projected, let alone built and in operation, that body was called upon to adjudicate in the delicate matter of rail gauges. Ireland certainly got off to a good start, with the Ulster Railway, incorporated in May 1836, building the first part of its line from Belfast to Armagh with a gauge of 6ft 2in, and the Dublin & Kingstown, dating from 1834, adopting 4ft 8½in. But it was when the Dublin & Drogheda, authorised in 1836, began construction on the 5ft 2in gauge 'there bid fair to be as many gauges in Ireland as there were counties', as E. L. Ahrons once expressed it. But the Ulster and the Drogheda lines realising that before long they would extend to make contact with each other referred the gauge question to the Board of Trade, with a farsightedness that was lacking in England at the time. For the year was then 1843, two years before the attitude of the Great Western precipitated the Battle of the Gauges. In Ireland what might have been just such another confrontation was avoided before matters had gone too far.

The chief inspecting officer of railways at the Board of Trade addressed a circular letter to most of the leading railway engineers of the day asking their opinion as to the ideal gauge, if a new start could be made uninhibited by existing constructions. Pointedly, however, Brunel was omitted, as being, in Irish parlance, somewhat 'beyond the pale', and the general

97

view was that the gauge should be not less than 5ft and not more than 5ft 6in. The Board of Trade thereupon split the difference, and authorised 5ft 3in for all railways in Ireland, definitely requiring the Ulster and the Dublin & Kingstown to alter their lines to agree. At that time the Ulster Railway had progressed no further out of Belfast than Portadown, 25 miles, and the Dublin & Kingstown was only six miles long, so that no great upheavals were caused by this edict from London. It was an equally simple matter to change the finished portion of the Dublin & Drogheda from 5ft 2in to 5ft 3in in time for its opening in May 1844.

In the ensuing three years a remarkably high porportion of the ultimate Irish standard (5ft 3in) gauge railway network was authorised, including the entire main lines of the Great Southern & Western (Dublin to Cork) and the Midland Great Western from Dublin to Galway. The line that eventually became the Dublin & South Eastern was authorised in 1846, as the Waterford, Wexford, Wicklow & Dublin, but this latter did not immediately get off the ground, and it was as the Dublin & Wicklow Railway, opened in 1856, that this line to the south began business. With its title changed to Dublin, Wicklow & Wexford in 1860 it eventually reached the last mentioned place in 1872. During this spate of Irish railway promotion, however, local circumstances were vastly different from those currently prevailing in England, when the Mania was just beginning to warm up to its full intensity. The economy of Ireland as a whole was based upon agriculture, and from 1846 for a few years there came the unmitigated disaster of the great potato famine. With the peasants reduced to near starvation by the non-existence of their staple food the death toll ultimately mounted to well over six figures. Between the larger towns, and there were not all that many of them, there was little to provide any intermediate traffic, except the pitiful flow of half-starved emigrants.

Yet the main lines were built, and many secondary ones, like the Londonderry & Enniskillen, the Newry & Armagh, the

Irish North Western from Dundalk to Enniskillen, and the Waterford & Limerick, which eventually extended its activities to the west coast at Sligo, saddled with a main line 222½ miles long, by far the greater part of which was single track. Moreover all this activity was on the 5ft 3in gauge, before any question arose of building the network of narrow gauge feeder lines, some of which were of such length, and such lifelines in the districts they traversed as to be called main lines. What became the busiest line in Ireland was that between Dublin and Belfast, and it was promoted, and for some time operated in three sections. There were the two originals whose difference in rail gauges led to the appeal to the Board of Trade in 1843; then to link them came the Dublin & Belfast Junction, incorporated in July 1845 to build a line from Drogheda to Newry, and a junction line to join the Ulster Railway at Portadown. The three links in the Dublin-Belfast main line were eventually amalgamated with the Irish North Western to form the Great Northern Railway of Ireland in 1876.

One of the most striking features of the railway map of Ireland as it was gradually built up is the absence of competing lines. No second company, or alliance of companies arose to fight for Dublin-Belfast traffic, just as the Great Southern & Western had the Dublin-Cork run to itself. The one exception, perhaps, was Londonderry, served from Belfast by both the Great Northern and the Belfast & Northern Counties. But there was very little through traffic between the two cities — nothing to stimulate building up of race conditions; the two routes served widely separated districts intermediately, with the GNR going through Dungannon, Omagh, and Strabane, and the BNCR serving Antrim, Ballymena, Ballymoney, and Coleraine. The latter was the shorter route, totalling 92¾ miles, after the opening of the Greenisland loop line in 1934, which made possible a much improved service to all points on the North Atlantic coast. Until then the Great Northern had the best of it over its route of 100½ miles, and journey times of

2 ¾ to 3 hours. Apart from this mild competition between Belfast and Londonderry the districts served by the principal Irish lines were as neatly parcelled out geographically as the railways of France.

Towards the end of the nineteenth century with the increase of tourism there was considerable competition between the English companies for traffic to and from Ireland, but a business of international importance developed on the Great Southern & Western, from the calling of trans-Atlantic liners, at Queenstown (now Cobh). It was found that by disembarking there, taking the train to Dublin, crossing thence to Holyhead, and travelling by LNWR much time could be saved on the journey to London, avoiding the delays often experienced in getting into the port of Liverpool, and from fogs in the Mersey estuary. This operation came into prominence at the time of the famous Trent case, during the American Civil War in 1861. The Queen's Messenger carrying the vital despatch from Washington in response to the British ultimatum was landed from the SS *Europa* by tender at Cork, whence the GS&WR ran a special train to Dublin. At that time, however, the City of Dublin Junction Railway had not been opened and conveyance between Kingsbridge (now Heuston) and Westland Row (now Pearse) stations in Dublin had to be by road.

By the turn of the century the Great Southern & Western had developed the American mail traffic into a regular prestige service. The Outward Mails, as they were known, carrying those from London and the continent of Europe not only for the USA and Canada, but also for Japan via Vancouver, were run regularly on Sundays and Thursdays; they carried mails picked up at Queenstown by the steamers that had left Liverpool for New York on the previous Wednesday and Saturday afternoons, the saving in time thus being several days before even the liner was joined. On the GS&WR these American specials were primarily mail trains, and were accorded priority over all other traffic on the line. They included a limited amount of luxurious passenger accommodation. By this service a New York correspondent could get a reply to a letter sent to London in eleven days— then an absolute world record! By the same time the GS&WR had introduced some excellent bogie corridor coaches and dining cars for both first and second class passengers, while in the tourist season special express trains were run between Dublin and Killarney. The long secondary main line westward from Mallow over which these trains run was opened as early as 1854.

At one time four English railways were involved in steamer services across the Irish Sea, namely the London & North Western, Midland, Lancashire & Yorkshire, and the Great Western. The first named, working in partnership with the City of Dublin Steam Packet Company held the contract for conveyance of the Royal Mail, but from Holyhead it also operated a service with its own steamers to Dublin, North Wall, and yet another service from Holyhead to Greenore, in a much favoured holiday district amid the Mountains of Mourne. The LNWR even had a subsidiary railway of its own, the Dundalk, Newry & Greenore, which connected with points on the Great Northern main line. The Midland entered Ulster in a big way, absorbing in its entirety the Belfast & Northern Counties Railway, which henceforth became known as the Northern Counties Committee section of the Midland. This merger was authorised in July 1903. At the same time as this notable expansion of territory a magnificently equipped new harbour was built at Heysham, from which the Midland's own steamers began to operate a nightly service to Belfast. It was then said that one could travel Midland all the way from London to Londonderry. The outward appearance of the former BNCR locomotives and rolling stock was not affected by this takeover, the locomotives remained a rather drab 'invisible green'. The only difference was that the initials on the tenders was changed from BNCR to NCC.

Despite the bounding enterprise of the Midland, however, the Royal Mail route to Northern Ireland lay via Fleetwood, and was the joint responsibility of the London & North Western and Lancashire & Yorkshire railways. The latter provided the steamers, which sailed to Belfast, and the connecting 5.30pm express from Euston was one of the really crack services of the LNWR. The Lancashire & Yorkshire also ran a nightly service from Liverpool to Drogheda. Even after the Midland had opened the new dock at Heysham harbour there were still sailings to Belfast from Barrow-in-Furness, and the evening Furness line express from Carnforth which brought through carriages from Euston and from Leeds was advertised as running in connection with the Belfast boat. While the Midland, the North Western, and the Lancashire & Yorkshire were all active across the Irish Sea the Great Western was making strenuous efforts to develop a very strong and profitable holiday traffic to the south of Ireland. The original route had been from New Milford to Waterford, but in June 1893 the Fishguard & Rosslare Railways & Harbours Company was incorporated, jointly by the Great Western and the Great Southern & Western. The board was composed of four directors of the GWR and three of the GS&WR. Its original Act, and subsequent authorisations covered the construction of splendid new harbours at Fishguard and at Rosslare, and construction of a length of new railway to connect from Rosslare to the existing GS&WR lines at Waterford.

Once this route was opened for traffic in August 1906, the partners began to flog it for all it was worth in developing traffic from England and Wales to the South of Ireland. It was in fact the shortest route to the famed beauty resorts in the west of County Kerry, and enterprise reached its zenith in September 1907 with the first of the day excursion trips from London to Killarney, worked by the Great Western in the late evening non-stop from Paddington to Fishguard. The Irish share in the enterprise was to run across the southern part of the country through Waterford, intersecting the main Dublin-Cork line at Mallow and then continuing west to Killarney, 154¼ miles on the GS&WR. This, however, was no more than one of the stunts organised by this new route. In connection with the overnight steamer from Fishguard there were boat expresses with breakfast cars for both Dublin and Cork. Of course the former provided a much slower overall service from London than that of the Irish Mail from Euston, via Holyhead, but it served Wexford and Wicklow, and many intermediate stations in that beautiful eastern side of Ireland before arriving in Dublin at 10.45am. The Cork boat train from Rosslare Harbour handsomely beat the main line connection from Dublin, off the regular Irish Mail, arriving at 10.03am.

At the turn of the century and thereafter the mail trains on all radiating lines from Dublin were so timed that even at the most distant points of the main lines, for example, Galway and Cork, letters from England would arrive in time for a reply to be got off by the up mails connecting with the Kingstown-Holyhead packet the same night. Although it is carrying the story into the 1930s the times of arrival and departure of the mails were 10.55am and 3.50pm at Cork, and 11am and 3.30pm at Galway. The Midland Great Western Railway, by which the latter service was maintained ran directly east to west across Ireland, with its principal stations at Mullingar, Athlone and Athenry. Even on its main line its running speeds were never very high, but within its own particular area it served an adequate purpose. It had long unremunerative extension lines, such as that from Athlone to Westport and Achill; from Mullingar to Sligo, and that extraordinary line that used to follow the road through the wilds of Connemara from Galway to Clifden, on which it was said that a donkey and a jaunting car could easily make better time than the train!

In the north, the Belfast & Northern Counties had a route handicap that was not eliminated until the 1930s. It had some steep climbing to do in getting across the high ridge that runs parallel to the western shores of Belfast Lough, and the original survey took the line at water level some distance towards Carrickfergus and then the line to Antrim,

Ballymena, and Londonderry climbed the ridge in a backward direction, as it were. A through train from Belfast thus had to reverse direction at Greenisland, involving a stop, attachment of a different engine at the opposite end of the train, and additional mileage. It is rather surprising that when the Midland Railway took over the line in 1903 it allowed this awkward location to remain. It lengthened the journey from Belfast to Antrim and places beyond by the best part of a quarter of an hour. The new direct line was built as one of the works undertaken for the relief of unemployment in the great slump of the early 1930s.

Although they were not main lines in the ordinary sense of the word the narrow gauge railways of Ireland provided for many years such a necessary feature of the transportation scheme in so many of the remoter districts that some reference to the more important ones is appropriate. Furthermore, one cannot entirely disregard the emotional fascination of these lines, even in a book like this, which is concerned mainly with the broad outlines of development. So, for a few paragraphs may I give myself up to the emotive charm of lines like the Ballycastle, the County Donegal, the Lough Swilly, and the Tralee & Dingle. It would have been good to read Ahrons on some of these lines. In his famous series of articles in *The Railway Magazine* he was at his wittiest in writing of the Irish broad gauge lines; but although he no doubt travelled on some of them he never wrote of the narrow gauge. These light railways, as they were officially termed, all built on the 3ft gauge, and which ran beside the public highways in many cases for miles on end, were authorised by a succession of Light Railways Acts, passed by Parliament in 1883, 1889, and 1896, and provided for state assistance, in certain cases of a free grant of half the cost of construction, if it were shown that a light railway was necessary for the development of a district.

The Ballycastle Railway when I travelled on it in 1935 was part of the NCC and its two locomotives and the coaching stock were resplendent in Midland red livery. It was no more

Above: GWR: a down stopping train, with a mixed collection of stock near the site of the present Old Oak Common locomotive and carriage depot. The locomotive is one of the Dean outside framed 2–4–0s, No 3224. *(L&GRP Collection)*

Below: Great Eastern Railway: a heavy Yarmouth express in 1901 on the steepest part of Brentwood bank, double-headed by Class T19 2–4–0 No 735 and a Claud Hamilton class 4–4–0 No 1892. *(L&GRP Collection)*

The way north from Carlisle.

Above: A Caledonian express hauled by a Dunalastair I class 4–4–0, No 733. *(L&GRP Collection)*
Below: St Pancras–Glasgow express hauled by one of the GSWR Manson 4–6–0s, No 383. *(L&GRP Collection)*

than 16¼ miles long, connecting with the main line at Ballymoney. Although sponsored by an independent company in 1878 the Belfast & Northern Counties Railway subscribed £18,000 towards the capital needed. It provided a regular passenger service, connecting with main line trains. When I travelled on it the working was on the one-engine-in-steam principle. Two of the interesting 2-4-2 two-cylinder compound tank engines of Bowman Malcolm's design were stationed at Ballycastle, and they worked the service on alternate days. The Ballycastle Railway had remained an independent company until 1924, when, after a short period of being closed altogether, it was taken over by the LMS, and placed under NCC management. The 2-4-2 tank engines were originally built for the Ballymena & Larne Railway, incorporated in 1874, but which was amalgamated with the B&NCR in 1889. It was the only narrow gauge line in Ireland over which an express train was ever run, though to be sure there were occasions elsewhere when express speeds were attained when narrow gauge trains got out of control on steep gradients! But the Ballymena & Larne ran a boat express in each direction, connecting with the steamer sailings across to Stranraer; they ran the 25¼ miles in the exact hour, inclusive of one intermediate stop. The service was discontinued from 1933.

At one time Londonderry was quite a remarkable railway centre. In addition to the broad gauge lines of the B&NC and Great Northern, it was the railhead of two of the most extensive narrow gauge systems in Ireland, the Londonderry & Lough Swilly with its associated Letterkenny & Burtonport Extension, and the County Donegal. To study a map of North-West Donegal, and to trace the one-time route of the Lough Swilly, and its Burtonport extension is to marvel that even a light 3ft gauge railway ever came to be built through such a wild, unproductive and sparsely populated countryside. The Burtonport extension alone was 49¾ miles long. It was authorised in 1898, with the Government of the day providing most of the capital as a free grant. The Lough Swilly itself

107

added another 49¾ miles of route, though not in quite such a remote countryside. Once built, however, the railway, providing a main line from Londonderry, was operated on strictly cheeseparing tactics, so that the track and rolling stock fell into a state of chronic disrepair. After World War I the only thing that kept the Burtonport extension in operation was that the roads were in such a shocking state as to preclude the use of any motor traffic that could offer competition! The trains, when one eventually hove in sight, were highly picturesque, and the motive power included some 4-8-4 tank engines and the only two tender engines on any Irish narrow gauge line, remarkably of the 4-8-0 type.

The railways of the County Donegal Joint Committee were no less remote. Today one can trace their one-time routes, beside the roads euphemistically described as 'trunk roads', from Strabane, with its connection to the Great Northern, to the first major junction at Stranorlar. From there, one line, to Glenties, followed the course of what even now is described as no more than a link road, while the second forced a way through the wild and desolate Barnesmore Gap to reach Atlantic tidewater at Donegal. Thence two winding, straggling extensions pressed on, one to Killybegs, farther west on the Atlantic coast, and the other southwards to Ballyshannon, through which a broad gauge line of the Great Northern passed, to reach the coastal resort of Bundoran. The history of the County Donegal is long and complicated. Part of it indeed began as a 5ft 3in line, and was afterwards converted to 3ft. But the system at its maximum extent was 125 miles long, the longest of any narrow gauge line in the British Isles. It was built at intervals between 1863 and 1909. One interesting point in its history is that most of its traffic, in what might be called its heyday, was directed towards the port of Londonderry, and originally this was transferred to the Great Northern at Strabane. To avoid the inconvenience of this break of gauge a new *narrow gauge* line was promoted, over this 14½ miles, and despite strong opposition from the Great

Northern at the prospect of loss of its traffic, authorisation was obtained in 1896 and the line opened in 1900. By another curious twist, this short narrow gauge line between Londonderry and Strabane became the sole property of the English Midland Railway—not even NCC—in 1906. In due course it became purely LMS!

CHAPTER 9

World War I and its Sequel

At the beginning of 1914 'Home Rails' collectively were a sound proposition for the careful investor in the stock market, and if there were one or two shaky areas, such as Chatham and Great Central ordinary, the rest, including the principal Irish lines, were pretty good. It is worth looking at the dividends that were paid in the last full year before 1914 because they formed a basis of subsequent reckoning.

DIVIDENDS PAID ON ORDINARY SHARES

English Trunk Lines:

Great Western	$5\frac{5}{8}$	per cent
London & South Western	$5\frac{3}{4}$	,,
London, Brighton & South Coast	5	,,
South Eastern	$3\frac{7}{8}$	,,
London, Chatham & Dover	NIL	
Great Eastern	$2\frac{1}{2}$	,,
Great Northern	$4\frac{3}{8}$	,,
London & North Western	$6\frac{1}{2}$	,,
Midland (Preferred Ord)	$2\frac{1}{2}$	,,
(Deferred Ord)	$3\frac{7}{8}$	,,
Great Central	NIL	
North Eastern	6	,,
Lancashire & Yorkshire	$4\frac{1}{8}$	,,

Scottish Trunk Lines:

Caledonian	$3\frac{3}{4}$	,,
Glasgow & South Western	$4\frac{7}{8}$	,,
North British	4	,,
Great North of Scotland	1	,,
Highland	$2\frac{1}{4}$	,,

Principal Irish Lines:

Great Northern	$5\frac{1}{4}$	,,
Great Southern & Western	5	,,
Midland Great Western	3	,,

Secondary Lines, England and Wales:

Furness	$1\frac{1}{2}$	,,
Hull & Barnsley	3	,,

Maryport & Carlisle	$5\frac{3}{4}$	,,
North Staffordshire	$4\frac{3}{8}$	,,
Rhymney	$8\frac{3}{4}$	,,
Taff Vale	$3\frac{3}{4}$	,,

It is sometimes said that the coming of war in August 1914 caught the British nation unprepared. This was true enough so far as public opinion was concerned, and our army, though the most highly professional of any in the world, was certainly very small and at first quite unsuited to the long years of trench warfare that ensued. But in certain other very important respects Great Britain was very much prepared. There had been several warnings to which men of experience and discernment readily enough took heed. In July 1911, for example, there came the dangerous German intervention at Agadir, Morocco, in what would ordinarily have been no more than a minor French colonial fracas. Although German intervention was quickly turned into a fiasco by the strong combined action of France and Great Britain, outspoken comments made at the time in both Paris and London left Germany very angry, and responsible men in England realised how near to war we had been. No more than a month later, the Under Secretary of State for War called a meeting with the general managers of six of the leading railways to consider transport problems in time of war, and a year later the Railway Executive Committee was set up under the nominal chairmanship of the President of the Board of Trade. Its early deliberations were in practice carried out under the Acting Chairman, Sir Frank Ree, General Manager of the London & North Western Railway. In any preparations for wartime traffic, and the sending of an army overseas it was realised that the London & South Western would occupy a key position. On the death of Sir Frank Ree in February 1914, H. A. Walker, General Manager of the LSWR from the beginning of 1912, was asked to take over the job.

When war actually came, in August 1914, the REC consisted of the General Managers of nine English railways and

111

one Scottish: GWR, LSWR, SE&CR, GNR, LNWR, Midland, GCR, NER, and LYR, with the Caledonian in Scotland. Later, the Brighton was added. The following announcement was made shortly after the outbreak of war:

The control of the railways has been taken over by the Government for the purpose of ensuring that the railways, locomotives, rolling stock, and staff shall be used as one complete unit in the best interests of the State for the movement of troops, stores and food supplies. The necessity for this action must at once become apparent when it is realised that certain ports, through which the bulk of our food supplies enter this country, may be closed for the purpose of such food supplies, and, in that event, the rolling stock, locomotives, etc. may have to be diverted to other lines for the purpose of serving other ports. The staff on each railway will remain under the same control as heretofore, and will receive their instructions through the same channels as in the past.

The Railway Magazine of September 1914 carried an editorial article entitled 'British Railways Nationalised', and operationally so it actually was. Their efficiency and flexibility in operational management was a godsend to the Government, firstly in the smoothness and relative secrecy with which the Expeditionary Force and all its equipment was concentrated, mainly upon Southampton, in readiness for transport across the Channel. The public, as a whole, had little realisation of what was going on, even in the 20 hours from 10pm on Friday, 21 August, when no fewer than 73 special trains arrived at Southampton, on an average one every quarter of an hour. These brought regiments from all over the country, and that it was done with so little disruption of ordinary traffic, in the height of what would ordinarily have been the holiday season was a magnificent co-operative effort of all the railways of Britain. Much, of course, had been done before that hectic weekend; indeed, in his first despatch from France, dated 7 September, the Commander in Chief, Sir John French, said that the concentration had been practically complete by the evening of Friday 21 August. Although not all available troops were in France by that time, judging by the volume of traffic still pouring into Southampton, Sir John French must have had a substantial force, for only two days later, on Sunday 23 August, he fought the Battle of Mons, and held up the German advance for many crucial hours.

Then in support of the coming war at sea demands upon the railways in quite a different direction began to develop. The mobilisation of the Royal Navy, and the concentration of its principal strength in home waters based the battle-cruiser squadron in the Firth of Forth, and the main battle fleet in the far north of Scotland. The defences of the great anchorage of Scapa Flow were not ready on the outbreak of war, and for a few anxious months the great armada of some two dozen battleships, and their attendant smaller craft, under the Commander-in-Chief, Sir John Jellicoe, led a dangerous nomadic existence. At once, however, there arose the matter of supplies. All of the ships were then coal fired, and were designed to use the best Welsh steam grades, and that coal had to be hauled from South Wales up to Thurso. Although the London & North Western, and Caledonian Railways had locomotives that could handle this traffic, unusual though it was for both of them in its volume and tonnage, it was another matter for the Highland, over whose lengthy and heavily graded main line much of it had to be conveyed. There developed also on the Highland an unprecedented traffic in service personnel and mails. That splendid railway was well enough used to dealing with a high density of passenger traffic during the summer and autumn holiday season, but it *was* a seasonal business, and the less than generous resources of the railway were deployed accordingly.

In the works at Inverness major repairs on locomotives and coaching stock were carried out during the winter months when traffic was at its lightest, and the only extra duties likely to arise were to provide engines and crews to propel snow ploughs! But in the autumn of 1914 engines that had been hard at work during the summer and falling due for repair were required to carry on, with increasing intensity, during the winter, and with absolutely no likelihood of a let-up. Furthermore, the normal traffic of the Highland had left it with no locomotives ideally suited to the working of heavy coal trains. Inverness was chosen as the site for a colossal ammunition store for the Grand Fleet, but what affected the Highland more perhaps than any of the larger railways was the fall in manpower. There were no such things as reserved occupations. Beside the railway at Inverness were the barracks of the Cameron Highlanders, and when it became known that Lochiel had undertaken to raise an extra battalion of that famous regiment and to command it himself in action, the men simply flocked to join, whether they were farmers, clerks, locomotive enginemen, signalmen, or anything else. The works became desperately short of fitters, and great difficulty was experienced in manning all the main line signal boxes. Amidst this sublime manifestation of patriotism the Highland was denied the use of six of the finest and most powerful locomotives that had yet taken the road in Scotland, through the arrogant intransigence of one senior officer, and the technical ignorance and pigheadedness of another—a sad reflection upon the frailty of human nature, even in the face of such an emergency. Through the centralised control of the REC the Highland managed to borrow a number of locomotives from other railways, and a few new ones were purchased, but it was a hard struggle for those in charge at Inverness.

At Government request the great railway workshops in England switched a considerable part of their equipment and resources to manufacture of munitions of war, but it was sometimes difficult to convince men in whom the fires of patriotism burned most fiercely that maintaining the locomotive stock in good shape was just as important a wartime task as the making of shells, gun mountings, or other direct munitions. At Crewe, for example, in 1915, when the men had felt that the resources of that great works should be switched more extensively, the Chief Mechanical Engineer, C. J. Bowen Cooke, addressed a mass meeting of his men, and explained why good locomotive maintenance was essential. When in 1915, they had passed a resolution: 'We, the working men of Crewe, will do all that is humanly possible to increase the output of munitions, and stand by our comrades in the trenches', Bowen Cooke had reminded them of the second part of their two-fold task: 'It is to those who produce the material for the making and repair of locomotives who have this all-important matter in their hands.' The sentiments at Crewe were paralleled in the other great railway works in Britain, though on not quite so intimate a basis, because few of the chief mechanical engineers were held in quite the same affectionate regard as was C. J. Bowen Cooke.

One of the less palatable effects of wartime conditions, so far as ordinary travellers were concerned, apart from reduction in frequency of service and deceleration of running times, was the rationalisation of travel, as to available routes. The case of London and the Scottish cities may be quoted as a major example. Before the War a traveller from London to Edinburgh had the choice of three routes, from Euston, St Pancras and King's Cross; but as war conditions developed to maximum intensity and austerity, bookings from London to Edinburgh were only permitted from King's Cross. Trains still ran on the one-time rival routes, but they were to provide services only from intermediate stations not served by the east coast route. To Glasgow facilities were shared by the Midland and west coast routes. In the morning, from London, a passenger for Glasgow could obtain a ticket only by the Midland route, and at midday only by the west coast. The deceleration, from the beginning of 1917 was intense, and when this was accompanied by the absence of any restaurant cars on long distance trains, and the inclusion of non-corridor coaches to provide more seating accommodation per tare weight of stock the privations of those whose journeys were really necessary can well be imagined!

The position of shareholders by the terms of the agreement by which the Government had taken control of the railways in 1914 meanwhile remained secure. The same dividends were paid as those of 1913, but there were some very disquieting trends. Costs were rising rapidly, and against a steep rise in the cost of living to more than double that of pre-war days, railwaymen had been awarded an additional war wage of 33s (£1.65) a week, which trebled the earnings of the lowest paid workers. Against this, passenger fares had been increased by no more than 50 per cent. There were the makings of trouble on this account, when Government control eventually ceased in 1921. At the same time the centralised control of operation exercised by the REC had made possible some notable economies, particularly in the elimination of competition in freight traffic. The position of coal supply for the country as a whole was so critical as to lead to the appointment of so eminent a transport man as Sir Guy Calthrop, General Manager of the LNWR, as Coal Controller; with Government authority behind him, he was able to do a mammoth job of rationalisation, ensuring that the needs of industry and of the Royal Navy were provided by the shortest possible hauls, instead of a situation that not infrequently existed in pre-war years of a coal producing area sending its products away to meet distant orders, while having to import supplies for its own needs.

There were of course some propagandists who claimed that Government control had improved the efficiency of the railways, and their officers; but the large number of railwaymen who were detached from their regular duties for those of high responsibility in special wartime Government service, while leaving sadly depleted staffs to carry on the immense task of running the railways, suggested that, as *The Railway*

Magazine remarked editorially: '. . . so far from the State improving the efficiency of railway officers, the course of the current war has proved beyond all question the capacity of railway officers to vastly increase the effectiveness of the State.'

With the ending of the war, the sudden release from all the tensions of the past four years, all the uncertainties arising from the end of munition production, and the demobilisation of the armed forces, led to mounting industrial unrest, particularly as rumours began to circulate that the Government was contemplating a reduction in railway wages. The problems that loomed ahead were particularly anxious for the Scottish railways whose wage levels had been considerably below those of the English companies in pre-war years, for local economic rather than discriminatory reasons. During the war, wage increases had been made on a national basis, and if, and when Government control ended the Scottish companies would have found the greatest difficulty in sustaining the prevalent rates. The unrest and uncertainty took a startlingly dramatic turn in September 1919, when the National Union of Railwaymen (NUR) called a general strike of all its members, so suddenly that at the outset neither the public nor an overwhelming body of the railwaymen had any clear idea of what it was about. Nevertheless ASLEF (the locomotivemen's union), though apparently having no grievance, called its own members out in sympathy.

Solid as was the initial response to the strike order, however, men began to return to work on the very first day, when the claims were seen to be so slight. Many thousands of men in non-railway service volunteered to help and in consequence train services all over the country were rapidly organised. Nevertheless the strike, the most serious that had then occurred in British railway history, went on for nine days. Eventually the concessions gained for the lowest grades, which were supposed to be the main reasons for the strike, were so small as to seem out of all proportion to the general dislocation, expense, and loss that had been caused. They amounted to no more than an increase of 2s (10p) per week, to bring the basic rate of the lowest paid up to 51s (£2.55), with a guarantee that the existing level of wages generally should continue up to the end of September 1920. The strike for the leaders of the railway unions was an expression of apprehension, rather than one of immediate grievance.

Earlier that year, the Act of Parliament setting up the new Ministry of Transport had received the Royal assent, and Sir Eric Geddes was appointed the first Minister of Transport; himself a railwayman of long experience, he had seen service on the Baltimore & Ohio, and in India, before joining the North Eastern in 1904. On that line he rose to become Deputy General Manager in 1911. During the war his services were at first loaned to the Ministry of Munitions, and in July 1917 he was appointed First Lord of the Admiralty. As Minister of Transport he had the delicate task of negotiating the transfer of the railways back from Government control to full private ownership, and having regard to the manifold advantages derived from the wartime co-operation between companies, and cognisant of the difficulty that was likely to arise in those companies with generally lower pre-war wage rates, on which their finance had been based, he evolved the great grouping scheme.

The original proposals for amalgamation discussed at the end of 1920 were very similar to those eventually adopted, but when the Bill was introduced into Parliament, it included provision for six groups, four English and two Scottish. There were to have been a West Scottish group, consisting of the Caledonian, Glasgow & South Western, and Highland, and an East Scottish group containing the North British and the Great North of Scotland. Very strong objection to this was immediately raised, because it would have perpetuated one of the difficulties left by Government Control, that of high wages in relation to the unchanged financial structure of the companies. The scheme was then amended to group the western Scottish companies with their natural and old-established English allies, and the eastern Scottish railways likewise. At one period during the committee stage of the Bill in the House of Commons there was a proposal to have a separate Midland group, to which the Glasgow & South Western would have been attached; but this proposal was quickly defeated, and the Bill that passed its third reading in the Commons contained the grouping arrangements that later became so familiar. It passed quickly through the House of Lords and so the Railways Act, 1921, received the Royal assent on 19 August 1921.

Whatever name may have been given to it, it was not 'grouping' in the truest sense of the word; nor could it have been in the very short time made available for discussion beforehand and during the committee stage in Parliament. The dominant factor was that on 15 August 1921, the railways were de-controlled, and it was imperative, as quickly as possible, to provide the legislation to enable post-war adjustment and development to be undertaken on the broadest possible basis. Nobody really liked the provisions of the Act, and it brought together some very unwelcome bed-fellows, but one sees now it was the best that could be done in the time. In England it left the anomaly of a number of joint railways, administered by two of the large groups. There was the Somerset & Dorset, for example, jointly owned by the LMS and the Southern; then there was the Midland & Great Northern Joint, almost entirely in the geographical territory of the new Eastern group, and joint lines of the Great Western and the LMS in the Welsh border country. Then again, although there was no case of joint ownership there was the interweaving of Midland and Great Central interests, with competitive lines, between London and Sheffield.

In Scotland, while the inclusion of the Caledonian and Glasgow & South Western in the LMS group removed one earlier source of fierce competition, the former areas of rivalry and overlapping between the Caledonian and the North British remained, together with perhaps the most outstanding anomaly of all, the inclusion of the West Highland and Mallaig Extension lines, together with the Invergarry and Fort Augustus branch, in the London & North Eastern Railway. To have handed these lines over to the Caledonian in 1921 would have created little short of a revolution, but the anomaly is enough to emphasise how the Railways Act of 1921 was a grouping of companies, rather than of territorial interests.

The LMS group had enough troubles on its hands without that of serious friction in Scotland. The managements of the former London & North Western, Midland, and Lancashire & Yorkshire Railways included many strong and able men, whose personalities clashed on matters of administration, engineering and operation, and there was a long drawn out period of friction, sparring for position, frustration and consequent lack of cohesion. Three great men whose sagacity in management and outstanding qualities as railwaymen were lost to the new combination by reason of their efforts in the war. Sir Guy Calthrop, and C. J. Bowen Cooke, respectively General Manager and Chief Mechanical Engineer of the LNWR, died in 1919 and 1920, and Cecil W. Paget, formerly Chief General Superintendent of the Midland, whose brilliant command of the Railway Operating Division of the British Army in France had won him a unique place in railway history, chose to enter the field of industry after the war, rather than return to railway service. It was not until the noted economist Sir Josiah Stamp was called in that the LMS became a truly cohesive and efficient organisation.

CHAPTER 10

The Fight to Modernise — Railways versus the Statute Book

Neither the main body of British railwaymen nor the onlookers could complain for lack of incident and variety in the first years after grouping. Everywhere partisanship for one or other of the pre-grouping companies ran high. There was anger and resentment over many of the major appointments, while decisions upon the future liveries of locomotives and coaching stock aroused strong feelings not only among the railwaymen most intimately concerned but amongst non-professional enthusiasts who had favoured one railway or another. Comparative trials of locomotives were conducted, and for good reason with no attendant publicity. The results, with appropriate partisan comments were leaked privately to one or two people, including the late Cecil J. Allen; but it was not until very many years later that the full authoritative results came to light, in many cases giving an entirely contrary view to the impressions that had been formed on earlier comments. The British Empire Exhibition staged at Wembley in 1924 and again in 1925 enabled the four groups to display their wares, and the rival publicity for the premier express passenger locomotives of the GWR and the recently formed London & North Eastern Railway was generally considered to have led to the Interchange Trials early in 1925, though as I have explained in other writings this was not directly the case.

The summer of 1925 was graced by the Railway Centenary celebrations at Darlington though there were some perfervid historians, as in 1975, who tilted at the name 'Railway Centenary' pointing out that there had been railways in many forms long before the opening of the Stockton & Darlington. But the glorious pageantry brought all the four groups together in a glow of pride of achievement and history. It was fortunate too, and highly appropriate to the occasion that the former North Eastern Railway had been to the fore in the preservation of historical locomotives, and for the special purpose of the pageant had restored two of its finest mid-19th century examples to their original condition and attendant finery of painting. Against this gracious setting, however, the clouds of industrial unrest were gathering again. There had been a lengthy coal strike in the spring and early summer of 1921 which hindered the railways in their attempts to get public services back to something near pre-war standards, but in 1925 the trouble went deeper. The coal owners, faced with dwindling returns sought to reduce their operating costs, either by a reduction in wages, or by longer hours for the same wages, and against such proposals the men stood foursquare in opposition.

The Government of Stanley Baldwin, faced with the prospect of another strike in the summer of 1925, bought time by setting up a Royal Commission to examine the mining industry, and at the same time paying a subsidy to the owners while the Commission was in session. The eight months respite enabled the forces of propaganda to get into action to enlist sympathy for the miners. When, in March 1926, the Coal Commission made its recommendations, and the miners rejected them out of hand the trade union movement as a whole was ready to support them; on May Day, the General Council of the Trade Union Congress decreed a General Strike. This, of course, brought out the railwaymen, but from the very outset the strike was never quite 'general'. Volunteers from all walks of life poured in with offers of help, and before long it was possible to run quite a number of trains. But although the so-called General Strike failed to paralyse the nation, as its architects hoped to do, and it was called off after nine days, the miners struggled on alone, and supplies of coal for the railways soon became critical. Arrangements were quickly made to import large quantities from the Continent,

Above: London & South Western Railway: a panoramic view of Queen Street station, Exeter, with locomotives ready to couple on to London expresses. *(L&GRP Collection)*

Below: Dover: the Admiralty pier, showing cross-Channel steamers berthed on both sides, and a South Eastern Railway boat train discharging passengers and luggage. *(Lambert Weston, Dover)*

Above: Somerset & Dorset Joint Railway: a southbound train on this cross-country mainline near Blandford, hauled by Derby style 4–4–0 locomotive No 14. *(L&GRP Collection)*

Below: London Tilbury & Southend Railway: a down Southend train, hauled by 4–4–2 tank engine No 44 *Prittlewell. (L&GRP Collection)*

while experiments were made with the oil firing of locomotives. The emergency, and the way it was met, was
important in showing the susceptibility of certain locomotive
design traditions to coal of a quality inferior to the very choice
grades on which design practice had previously been based.
Unfortunately in this respect, the emergency did not last long
enough for the lessons to be fully appreciated; when numerous
regional agreements, made successively in the autumn of 1926,
brought a virtual end to the coal strike before Christmas the
old conditions were largely restored. They did not arise again
until the far more serious disruption caused by World War II.

In the later 1920s it was evident that certain social and
economic trends were arising which would have a serious effect
upon railway viability. The grouping of the railways had so far
done little to effect economies in operation, in some directions
rather the reverse. With many of the old companies working in
closely defined geographical areas, harmonious and profitable
working arrangements existed between district representatives
of the railways, the latter being men well known and
respected, and entrusted by their superiors with authority to
make local deals. Their experience and knowledge of the
traffic in the areas made these profitable to all sides. But with
grouping, authority was in many cases transferred to remote
headquarters officials, who not only did not have their fingers
on the pulse of local affairs, but who inevitably took some time
to give decisions on questions put to them. This soon proved of
great annoyance to local traders, and unfortunately it came at
a time when the convenience of rail transport for small consignments from small town and country stations was being
seriously challenged. For reasons connected with the original
construction of the railways, many of the stations were not well
situated for local requirements, and road transport could
frequently offer an attractive and speedier alternative.

The average British main line goods train around 1930 was
an incredibly slow means of transport. It is true that all four of
the group railways ran a few fast freights, fully, or partially

fitted with continuous brakes, but the vast majority of goods trains were made up of loose-coupled four-wheeled wagons, which not only compelled relatively slow speeds when out on the open road, but which in the descent of any steep gradient made it essential to stop and pin down hand brakes on the wagons before beginning the descent, and to stop to release them afterwards. Even on the highways of the period with the vehicles then available, road transport could give much faster service, as well as providing door to door service. The railways soldiered on as best they could but it is significant of the modest demands made on locomotive power in freight service that the notable developments in construction during the later 1920s when there was competition between the companies to possess the most powerful locomotive should have been entirely for passenger service. This was in striking contrast to current developments in the USA, where freight engines of colossal size were being introduced. It must nevertheless be recorded that in British passenger locomotive design notable improvements in detail had resulted in very worthwhile reductions in basic fuel consumption. By 1930, however, except on the Great Western Railway the number of locomotives coming within this category was still relatively few, in relation to the total locomotive stocks.

The great slump of the early 1930s hit the railways hard, but one of the great handicaps under which they laboured was the legislation that regulated all their operations. They were common carriers. As such they were required by law to accept any traffic that was offered to them, and by 1930 that meant that they were being left with the least attractive and least remunerative jobs. The charges they could levy were regulated by legislation framed in a very different age, and the attitude that was gradually developing in the country as a whole was that railways were an out-of-date and inefficient form of transport. In the bad days of the slump, when money was generally tight, people found that they could travel much cheaper by long distance motorcoach. It was cash that counted. Less comfort en route and longer journey times counted for little against the attractions of lower fares.

Against this worsening situation the four railways fought back resolutely. The Southern, under the dynamic leadership of Sir Herbert Walker, its General Manager, determined on a policy of main line electrification, to the extent that the geography of their network permitted. It was not a long distance operation, but rather so many long extensions of the suburban system, using the same system of traction, low voltage direct current with third-rail pick up. The first line to be so equipped was that to Brighton, followed by extensions to Eastbourne and to Worthing. This was planned to be followed by conversion of the two alternative routes to Portsmouth. There is no doubt that the planning of the new services, with frequent-interval fast trains and new commodious coaching stock took the public fancy, and brought welcome increases in traffic. In the 1930s there was a growing desire of City workers to reside out of London, and with attractive season ticket rates, many with daily business in London travelled regularly from as far as the Sussex coast towns.

The Great Western was undoubtedly the most favourably situated of the four groups so far as continuing revenue was concerned, and its attitude to the changing trends was more conservative. It had of course been least affected by the grouping of 1923. It had been amalgamated with the larger of the local railways in South Wales, and had absorbed the others; although the effects of the prolonged coal strike in 1926 had been catastrophic, in the loss of overseas markets and export trade through the many fine docks that came under its administration in 1923, the business of the railway as a whole was so diversified that the local storm could be weathered. The railways of South Wales, although they had lost most of their proud identity and individualism in the grouping, had every reason to be thankful that in 1926 they were under the umbrella of the Great Western, otherwise lines like the Taff Vale, the Rhymney and the Barry, which depended so overwhelmingly on the coal trade, could have been utterly ruined. The Great Western made a brave show in accelerating certain selected express passenger trains, notably the Cheltenham Flyer, between Swindon and Paddington with a start-to-stop average speed of 71.4mph; although this brought little if any additional revenue, it was a prestige effort of the greatest importance to the image of the GWR and to the British railways as a whole.

On the LMS Sir Josiah Stamp, following many statistical analyses of working expenses, and noting that the locomotive department, in all its varying aspects, was by far the biggest spender, decided on a thorough-going reform of everything to do with traction. The company had inherited from six major railways and many more smaller ones a great diversity of locomotive designs of varying effectiveness and efficiency. Loyalty to the pre-grouping companies remained strong among all grades of the staff, and strong cases were made for the retention in first class service of this or that pre-grouping design. With the outlook of an economist and statistician rather than that of a traditional locomotive engineer, Stamp introduced a system of individual costing whereby every locomotive on the line and every penny spent on its maintenance and repair was individually recorded. At first some of the older men regarded this exercise as 'statistics run mad', but before long it was generally agreed that Stamp had forged a magnificent tool of management, which immediately separated out the sheep from the goats—and by the standards of the day the LMS did not have very many sheep! It became clear that a very high proportion of the total existing stock was urgently due for replacement. The problem which then presented itself was one of senior engineering management.

When Stamp took up his appointment on the LMS in 1926, partisanship within the locomotive department was at its height, with the principal factions representing the former London & North Western and Midland railways. There were also cross-currents involving the Caledonian and Highland railways. Matters had become more quiescent by 1930 when, in consequence of a change of status for Sir Henry Fowler, hitherto Chief Mechanical Engineer, a former Carriage & Wagon man, E. J. H. Lemon, was appointed to succeed him, largely in a caretaker capacity. Stamp was convinced that the only way to secure the cohesion necessary to achieve the major programme of locomotive replacement needed was to bring in a complete outsider, but one with the human qualities of leadership in addition to first rate technical and managerial ability. The choice fell on W. A. Stanier, then Principal Assistant to the Chief Mechanical Engineer of the GWR, and it could not have been a better one. With a mandate to 'scrap and build', providing a range of entirely new locomotives of the minimum number of different types, that would run longer weekly mileages, need the minimum of intermediate repairs, and be economical in fuel and oil consumption, Stanier's monumental work enabled traffic to be operated with many fewer locomotives, and at a much reduced bill for fuel and repairs. Moreover he built, personnel wise, for the future, gathering around him a team of engineers who were to carry on the traditions he established on the LMS to the very end of the steam era in Great Britain, some 30 years after he had taken office in January 1932.

In the austere times that succeeded the worst years of the great depression there were some gracious occasions to be celebrated. In 1935 there came a double event, one for the British Empire in its entirety, in the Silver Jubilee of King George the Fifth's reign, and the second, also under Royal patronage, was a family occasion for the Great Western, the Centenary of its incorporation. The 25th anniversary of the King's accession came in May; the famous high-speed stream-lined train that bore its name did not take to the road until September, but then in a blaze of justifiable publicity that was appropriate to such a successful innovation. The Great Western introduced another fast train, The Bristolian, as part of its centenary celebrations. This, like the Silver Jubilee train of the LNER, although bringing some welcome publicity to the railways did not contribute more than a widow's mite to the rather grim balance sheets of the day, though both trains are important in marking definite breakaways from traditional British express train operation. They were trains of fixed formation, relatively light, and run at speeds considerably higher than the general standards of passenger service then provided. That they were technical embarrassments in other directions than the mere provision of the necessary tractive power is apart from the point at this stage. Their true significance lay in the evidence provided that the business community appreciated higher speed, and would have been prepared to patronise many more trains of that kind. Investigations towards the provision of a similar service to The Bristolian on the London-Birmingham-Wolverhampton route of the GWR proved abortive however.

Apart from these isolated, if spectacular spurts in the passenger field the railway situation was generally sombre, and the first attempts to secure any relief from age-old legislation that hamstrung much of their operations in freight traffic met with little response—rather the reverse in fact. Indeed the trend that had begun earlier of a gradual transfer to road haulage became much more pronounced. The road hauliers, entirely free of the restrictions that hampered much of railway freight working took the cream of the traffic, and to a large extent the railways were left with the business that no one else wanted. The road hauliers on the other hand also operated under financial conditions that were much more favourable, in that they contributed very little towards the upkeep of the roads they used. To crown all, of course, the railways were always fair game for critics in the press and in Parliament, and any attempt to secure for them relaxations to enable them to compete on equality instantly met with implacable opposition. It was a disturbing and unhappy time for railway management.

Then, while another splendid Imperial celebration was on

hand, the Coronation of King George the Sixth in 1937, a factor more disturbing even than loss of revenue in freight traffic began to arise. At that very time the participation of the Fascist countries in the Spanish Civil War, and the use of the weapon of propaganda with a sickening disregard for the truth by both Germany and Italy, led the hitherto unthinkable prospect of a second world war to loom up in the minds of many people in Great Britain. How seriously this prospect was being taken, as early as 1937, was shown by the setting up of a Railway Technical Committee, to report upon the measures that should be taken to protect the lines, and keep traffic moving during emergencies. One thing was clear. In any future war aerial bombardment would take a prominent place. The Spanish Civil War had shown the kind of devastating attacks that might be expected. The committee worked with a sense of urgency, all the more necessary as the next act of Nazi aggression — the Austrian coup — came early in 1938. By that time men and women of every estate were volunteering for various forms of civil defence, because with the passing of every week the situation grew ever more ominous, with the flashpoint centred upon Czechoslovakia. Surreptitiously at first, arrangements for air raid precautions were initiated on the railways.

At the same time, however, preparations were being made for the square deal campaign to try and secure, by enlisting public sympathy, the necessary support for changes in legislation over the fixing of rates and fares, and to make the railways more competitive. Preparations were well advanced by the summer of 1938, but with the international situation deteriorating so rapidly the launching of the campaign was delayed. We came very near to war in the early autumn of that year, and while Neville Chamberlain then Prime Minister, was engaged in his personal discussions with Hitler, the Minister of Transport appointed a new Railway Executive Committee, at first in no more than an advisory capacity, and consisting of the general managers of the four grouped railways and Frank

Pick of the London Passenger Transport Board. Although the immediate crisis was ended with the notorious Munich agreement on 4 October 1938, very few men in high authority were convinced that it was really 'Peace in our time', and indeed the REC was instructed to press on with its emergency plans with *increased* vigour! Whatever may have been said in public, or printed in the newspapers, Neville Chamberlain had bought the railways, the armed forces, and the British Empire as a whole an absolutely vital eleven months to prepare for the worst, for which humanity can never cease to be grateful.

When the immediate international crisis was over, the railways pressed ahead with the square deal campaign, which was launched in earnest in November with urgent representations to the Minister of Transport, and wide publicity at principal stations and in all the national newspapers. *The Railway Gazette* commented editorially on November 25:

> The events of the recent crisis showed clearly that in any period of national emergency the railways would be indispensable, as road transport could not possibly cope with the services which the railways would be called upon to perform. Further, the railways can fairly claim that they have been largely instrumental in building up the country's export and import trade upon which we so greatly depend. Is it unreasonable, therefore, that they should seek the same freedom from Parliamentary control of their charges and conditions of carriage as is enjoyed by all other transport concerns and particularly road hauliers? It cannot be reiterated too strongly that the companies do not seek preferential treatment. The plain fact is that they are being gravely injured by the one-sided control of their charges for the conveyance of merchandise, and serious national reactions must inevitably follow if they are denied the right to compete on equal terms with other forms of transport.

It must be recorded, however, that the square deal

campaign met with a generally hostile press. The road haulage lobby was very strong in Parliament, and although the British Road Federation gave qualified support at first, the negotiations with the Ministry of Transport were protracted, and eventually overshadowed by the deepening crisis over the threats to Poland. After the end of the General Strike in 1926 there had been industrial peace on the railways, but in 1939 the unions felt that with improving traffic the time had come to submit a revised pay claim. The situation had to some extent been stirred up by Nazi propaganda in gibes and sneers against conditions of work on British railways—coming ill from the leaders of a mercilessly exploited police state. The unions met the railway companies in mid-August 1939, and agreed to differ. But while the NUR agreed to submit its claim to the Railway Staff National Tribunal, the leaders of ASLEF, with characteristic militancy declared a general strike of its members from midnight, 26 August! Now, as then, it seemed an incredible attitude. The Nazi war of nerves against Poland was reaching its climax. Germany had been warned categorically that any attack on Poland would be met by instant intervention by Great Britain and France. There were no ifs and buts about it; war could be upon us at any minute. Yet Britain had a strike of locomotive men definitely chalked up on the national agenda!

It was plain humanity rather than any softening of the implacable façade of ASLEF policy that dispersed this deplorable prospect. At a meeting with the Minister of Labour, Ernest Bevin on 24 August, an appeal was made to the ASLEF Executive Committee: 'We may need you to get the children away', and left to themselves afterwards the Executive agreed to call off the strike and follow the lead of the NUR in submitting their case to arbitration. But it was a close-run thing, and an unsavoury cliffhanger of an episode coming at the end of an era that left some very mixed memories.

CHAPTER 11

World War II — Greatest Task Ever

Some years ago when I wrote a full length book on the part played by Britain's railways during the war of 1939-1945, my concluding sentence was: 'In plain terms, the cumulative effort of the British railways over the years 1940-1945 represents the greatest achievement in railway transportation in the history of the world.' Re-reading that book today, far from feeling any need to qualify that final sentence, I would underline it heavily. In the present survey, covering the history of 150 years of working, I have space for no more than a single chapter about those apocalyptic years, and can refer only to salient features rather than the countless points of detail that arouse such heart-warming reflections. When war was declared on Sunday 3 September 1939, those of us who were connected in any way with the railways had scarcely recovered from the shock of ten days earlier, when in the face of an imminent and terrible national emergency it had been evident that the leaders of ASLEF were prepared to put the railway system of the country at hazard. It was so utterly at variance with the spirit of railwaymen generally in the years that followed, against that most inhibiting of violent enemy action — that in which the recipient has no direct means of hitting back.

Rather than attempt to trace the story of those 6½ years chronologically, which would be difficult and unsatisfactory in a single chapter I have divided the subject into five broad sections, to emphasise great overall issues:

1 Organisation for war
2 Train services and their changes
3 Dealing with sudden emergencies

4 Wagon stock control

5 D-day and after.

Two days before the actual declaration of war, the Government put the railways under the executive control of the Railway Executive Committee, composed of the General Managers of the four main line railways, Frank Pick, representing the LPTB and V. M. Barrington-Ward of the LNER, who was Chairman of the Operating Committee of the REC. The Chairman was Sir Ralph Wedgwood, recently retired from the general managership of the LNER. Because of the expectancy of heavy bombing attacks, the disused deep level tube station of Down Street, on the London Transport's Piccadilly Line, was adopted as REC headquarters. The decision to use it was taken in March 1939, and although there was a great amount of structural work to make it adequate for its vital task, the Committee, and its staff were able to occupy it from the outbreak of war.

Down Street became the nerve centre of the entire control of the British railways, and as the operations became increasingly complex so central co-ordination grew more and more important. This is not to say that matters were taken out of the hands of the men on the spot, at such vital operating centres as Crewe, Bristol, Derby, or York; far from it, because the officers in charge at these points very often had to improvise at a moment's notice. There was no question of ringing up headquarters and asking what was to be done. Since grouping, much had been done to extend the control system of traffic regulation. On the LMS the system of the former Midland Railway initiated by Sir Cecil Paget had been adopted generally with conspicuous success. On the LNER however the virtual autonomy granted to the three Areas had resulted in different practices within the railway. In the Southern Area, where V. M. Barrington-Ward was Operating Superintendent, the Midland system had been adopted. 'B-W', as he was always known on the line, had been a senior officer on Paget's staff in the ROD during World War I, and was completely converted to his methods, whereas in the North Eastern and Scottish Areas the train graph system was used, and I may add, with equal success.

At the outbreak of war it had been anticipated that widespread and severe bombing would start at once, and all four groups brought into effect emergency timetables, between 25 September and 16 October. The frequency of service was drastically reduced and booked speeds even more so. The parameters laid down by the REC were that no point-to-point times giving speeds of more than 45mph were to be booked, and to reduce track and rolling stock maintenance to a minimum an overall speed limit of 60mph was imposed. These exceedingly drastic curtailments were a measure of the expectancy of severe dislocation that was anticipated in the early days of the war. That heavy bombing did not come until many months later was fortunate, in that the respite enabled railwaymen of all grades to get used to working under blackout and other wartime conditions, and in taking the measure of passenger and service personnel travel to introduce considerable and welcome improvements in the train services. Nevertheless, all dining cars remained withdrawn, though the discomforts of travelling at night had been greatly relieved by improved lighting behind the blackout screens in the carriages.

By 4 December 1939 the maximum speed limit was relaxed from 60 to 75mph, and this remained the maximum for the rest of the war. Some acceleration of train services became possible, though the trains themselves were becoming much more crowded. With more than a million men undergoing military training and many more drafts on the way, the number of men and women in uniform travelling by train was constantly increasing. When travelling to training camps, medical boards, depots and on leave, members of His Majesty's forces were issued with railway warrants which were exchanged at the stations for railway tickets. On long journeys, warrants were also issued to enable such men and women to obtain meals at special prices in the railway refreshment rooms. Therein, the work of the staffs at the larger stations was beyond praise. Trains of gargantuan length, packed from end to end, would arrive at all hours of the day and night; there would be a concerted dash for the refreshment rooms, and then the speed, efficiency and good humour with which stalwart women of all ages coped with successions of such invasions was marvellous. There could be no finer manifestation of the spirit of Britain in those days than the Crewe refreshment rooms dealing with the brief halt of an Anglo-Scottish express in the middle of the night!

While all the discomforts of travel during the war were, for the most part, cheerfully borne by those civilians who had to travel, one facet of Government control came frequently under justifiable criticism. Everyone who had any perception at all realised that the railways had a colossal task on hand, and as the war went on the public was frequently assailed by poster and other means of propaganda: 'Is your journey really necessary?', 'Give your seat to a shell', and so on. But in every crisis in the war, when it was essential to limit civilian travel to the absolute minimum, the Ministry of War Transport relied upon exhortation, rather than the simple and obvious remedy of travel rationing. After all, everything else was rationed, so why not civilian rail travel? Ironically enough, the most unpleasant and serious consequence of this attitude came just when we were at last well on the way to winning the war, at the time of D-Day landings and immediately thereafter. With a view to keeping the lines as clear as possible for traffic to the Channel ports, and because of the expected counter-attacks on our supply lines, the railways were given strict instructions from the Ministry of War Transport not only to run no extra trains, but also not to strengthen any regularly scheduled trains, even to the extent of a single coach. Exhortations not to travel went forth as usual, and these might just have had the desired effect had not the enemy, at that very moment, been ready to launch the flying bomb attack on South-East England. In normal circumstances it would have been the summer holiday season and in the face of this alarming and unpredictable danger larger numbers of people, particularly from London, sought to get away. This sudden rush plus the Government embargo on the running of any additional coaches over the fixed formation of trains produced chaotic results.

The appalling danger, in the prevailing circumstances brought a characteristically forthright comment from the *Daily Mail:*

The Government gets no congratulations for the way it is handling the flying-bomb warning system or the rush to the railways.

For the first time in its history Paddington Station was closed (on Saturday) for some hours. The crowds were so large that they had to be controlled by mounted police. We hesitate to think what the casualty list might have been had a flying bomb fallen there.

This problem has cropped up every year, and every year the authorities have appeared to be bankrupt of ideas to solve it. Their only expedient has been to announce that no extra facilities will be made available to the travelling public.

On the same theme *The Railway Gazette* said:

It is regrettable that, notwithstanding its competence in other directions, the Ministry of War Transport has not shone in its dealings with passenger rail traffic. The same trouble has occurred at every holiday period during the war. Whilst refusing consistently to take any step to ration travel, it failed to give the railways a free hand to cope with any situation that might arise. It has contented itself with appeals and admonitions regarding unnecessary travel, apparently hoping that a Government Department would accomplish what no one else had succeeded in doing, namely, getting a quart in a pint pot.

Superlative examples of what the railway operating and engineering departments could do when given their heads were provided by the evacuation of the children immediately at the outbreak of war, the provision and running of trains for evacuation of troops of the British Expeditionary Force brought to the Channel ports from the beaches of Dunkirk, and in incredibly rapid repair of air raid damage on the lines during the Blitz, of 1940-1, and still more during the flying bomb and V2 rocket attacks.

The evacuation of the children was a superb example of operational planning, in which no fewer than 607,635 persons were taken out of London in the four days 1-4 September. When the scheme was drawn up it was envisaged that it might have to be carried out in conditions of continuous air attack, and the plan was to convey the children, in the charge of their teachers either by special trains of the LPTB or by buses, to outer London stations on the main line railways, where special long distance trains would take them to the relatively safe reception areas. The four stations chosen were Ealing Broadway, Wimbledon, Watford Junction and Bowes Park. On the main lines ordinary services had to be drastically curtailed to provide paths for so many specials, and to release and make available the coaching stock and locomotives to form them. Actually the disruption was relatively small, because in those last days before the outbreak of war ordinary business was virtually at a standstill. It was a magnificent feat of timing and organisation, so programming the arrival of evacuees at the main line stations that the time of transport of each party was kept to a minimum, and the youthful passengers whisked away without any protracted periods of waiting. Although in this same period there were considerable evacuations from Glasgow, Manchester and Merseyside, no fewer than 1577 special trains were run from the London area alone in those four days.

Dunkirk, of course, was in a different category altogether. In France, by the third week of May 1940 a force of some

300,000 men was being encircled and driven towards the sea by vastly greater enemy forces. An incredible armada of some 870 vessels from every harbour in the land was making for the Straits of Dover, including warships, railway steamers, pleasure craft, private cabin cruisers, yachts and small coastal motorboards. The Railway Executive Committee received a single instruction, to clear the British and Allied troops from the Channel ports, as fast as the Royal Navy and its associated armada could ferry them across from France. No one knew for certain at what rate troops would be landed, and where. There was no data to work upon, and no time to prepare written, let alone printed instructions. Everything had to be done by telephone. The operation was given the code name 'Dynamo' and a special control centre set up at Redhill, where military and railway officers worked in one gigantic combined operation. Before anything definite was known of actual numbers coming across, a pool of 186 trains were formed, of which the Great Western provided 40, the LMS 44, the LNER 47, and the Southern 55. They were made up into rakes of 10 coaches, so that they could be readily hauled by any locomotive available. As it turned out many of the specials were hauled away from the Channel ports by ex-SECR 4-4-0s from Tonbridge shed.

An extraordinary feature of the great evacuation as it proceeded was that it was completely unmolested by air attack on the English side of the Channel. The retreat to Dunkirk had been severely harassed by bombing of all kinds; the beaches had been raked by machine gun fire, and the quays where stretcher cases were being taken aboard hospital ships strafed unmercifully; and yet on a railway network particularly susceptible to air raid damage, in its many tunnels, and such a conspicuous target as the Foord viaduct at Folkestone, no damage at all was either attempted or inflicted. Between 27 May and 4 June, 565 special trains were run, conveying no fewer than 294,948 officers and men, and the actual points of departure were 327 from Dover, 64 from Folkestone, 82 from

Above: The Bournemouth Belle near Winchfield in the late 1940s hauled by Bulleid 4–6–2 No 21C15 *Rotterdam Lloyd*. *(M. W. Earley)*
Below: Euston–Glasgow sleeping car express of the late 1950s climbing Beattock bank in the early morning. The locomotive is 4–6–2 No 46256 *Sir William A. Stanier F.R.S.*, with bank engine in rear. *(W. J. V. Anderson)*

Above: A memory of 1937: the LNER streamlined Edinburgh–Kings Cross Coronation express at Low Fell hauled by A4 Pacific No 4487 *Sea Eagle*. (*The late W.B. Greenfield*)

Below: Western Region: the Cornish Riviera Express hauled by GWR 4–6–0 No 6000 *King George V* emerging from Sonning Cutting. (*M. W. Earley*)

Ramsgate, 75 from Margate and 17 from Sheerness. The work of the railwaymen was tremendous. While signalmen in the interests of safety were not asked to work longer than their normal shifts, the train crews worked incredibly long hours, and the control staff at Redhill, directing the whole operation by telephone, worked wonders of successful improvisation. Redhill was not only the control nerve centre of Operation Dynamo, it was the 'grand junction' from where trains were distributed on to lines for all parts of the kingdom. There was no time for engines to return to their own sheds. They were recoaled, and watered at Redhill, fires were cleaned, and smokebox ash shovelled out into the six-foot. No time was wasted queueing up for the turntable; engines returned to Dover tender first. Additional supplies of locomotive coal had to be worked to Redhill, while special wagons had to be arranged to clear the ash dumped from smokeboxes and fireboxes. Never in a thousand years of the stormy history of these Islands did the British genius for improvisation come more dramatically to our aid!

When the night blitz started in earnest, railwaymen faced a situation never previously encountered in British history. The men of the civil engineering departments went out in a spirit of battle valour to the repair of air raid damage on the line. There was no waiting for the raid to be over, still less for daylight to come in the short winter days. The gangs went out the moment they were advised of damage, and in many cases restoration of normal facilities took place in 24 hours. The resilience of all grades of railway staff was immediate and unceasing, and it was that marvellous spirit of wholehearted determination that enabled those responsible for impromptu planning to do so in the confidence that the response of the men would be immediate. But there were other railwaymen whose duties involved little in the way of valiant endeavour in the way of direct action. Think of a signalman alone in a small box, albeit controlling a vital junction when bombs were falling all around. Think again of the driver and fireman of a night express, leaving their homes in London just as a bad raid was beginning, and calmly working down the line on some long double-home duty, and inevitably anxious as to how their families were faring. The thousands of railwaymen who worked steadily in such circumstances showed a courage that was sublime. Many bomb stories were related in contemporary literature, some serious and causing grievous loss of life; in total effect the enemy caused an almost negligible hindrance to the working of the railways of Britain during the war, largely due to the courage, resolution, and resilience of the staff, of all grades.

Against the breathless haste, improvisation, and excitements of death-dealing incidents referred to earlier in this chapter, there was a humdrum, insidious malaise in operation on British railways that could, if not resolutely tackled, have proved a far greater handicap than direct enemy action. That was the control of wagon movement. At the outbreak of war there were 652,000 railway owned wagons in circulation, and no fewer than 585,000 wagons that were privately owned. While a number of these latter had been designed to carry specialised traffic a very large number were of the conventional open four-wheeled type owned by individual collieries and coal merchants. By the very nature of this ownership they spent nearly half their time running empty or standing in yards. At any time this was uneconomic from the railway point of view, because the haulage of empty wagons was unproductive and wasteful in locomotive power. Of course pre-war rates for transport of coal had naturally been framed to cover the cost of hauling empties back to the points of origin, but in the kind of war situation that was developing in 1940-1 any wagon running empty represented wasteful line occupation, if nothing worse. On the outbreak of war the 585,000 privately-owned wagons were requisitioned by the Government, but this did not solve the difficulty in avoiding empty running, and in March 1941 the Inter-Company Freight Rolling Stock Control was set up, at Amersham.

Its first task was the staggering one of establishing a routine procedure that would keep the new control centre supplied with an up-to-the-minute picture of the wagon situation throughout the country. The daily situation reports were to be divided into two categories, the first covering coal and coke, and the second general merchandise. In the latter case every station—*every station* in Great Britain!—was instructed to submit a daily return of the total number of wagons handled and their sub-classifications. At the same time stations were required to submit their needs for wagons, sheets and ropes for the following day. Although it was not to be expected that Amersham control would be able to meet every demand for wagons, with little more than 12 hours notice, the great point was that they were made aware of every traffic situation from day to day, and once the new Control got fully into its stride very few consignments were kept waiting for wagons for many hours. The railways of Britain had indeed been called upon for a phenomenal increase in output, as measured by the net ton-miles of all freight hauled. By 1943 this had increased by 46 per cent over the average of the last pre-war years; this increase had been obtained without any appreciable increase in rolling stock and fixed equipment, and despite the fact that 105,000 men and 4000 women had been released from the railway staffs for national service of various kinds. And it is only necessary to add that this astonishing increase had been secured despite all the hazards of wartime working, air raid damage on the lines and to railwaymen's homes. It was colossal!

In preparation for the great assaults of D-Day numerous small but significant improvements were made to track layouts on the British railways. Additional running lines were laid down north of Carlisle to obviate the two-line bottleneck over the River Eden. The line between Gloucester and Cheltenham was quadrupled, and many running loops were lengthened to accommodate the heavy freight trains that would require to be run. It was generally expected that when the invasion was

145

launched there would be heavy air attacks to damage and delay traffic to the ports of embarkation, and very careful provision was made for alternative routes, particularly on the lines leading to Southampton. It was in this context that the Didcot, Newbury & Southampton line, single-track to its junction with the Southern main line south of Winchester, was substantially up-graded. As things eventuated retaliation left the approaches to the invasion ports almost untouched, and took the form of yet another attack upon the civilian population, first with flying bombs, and then with the V2 rockets. Damage from these, around London, gave railway civil engineers some of their most difficult repair jobs, but the trains continued to go through.

Some of the most interesting work from the railway operating point of view, in the later stages of the war, concerned the build-up of great military strength in Great Britain prior to D-Day. By the end of 1943 the number of special trains required by the Government was averaging 250 a day! The order for them was often given to the railways at very short notice, and because many were concerned with the arrival of American troops there were often occasions when carefully planned arrangements had to be changed at the last moment, because of conditions at sea, the risk of U-boat attacks and so on. One might have the case of a convoy expected to arrive in the Clyde being switched to the Mersey instead. Anyone having no more than the vaguest ideas about railway operation can imagine what would be involved if all the coaches, wagons, vans and other vehicles that had been concentrated at Gourock, for example, had suddenly to be moved to Liverpool. Many trains could be required for a single ship. The Cunard White Star liner *Queen Elizabeth* brought the Americans over, with all their equipment, a division at a time.

It was not only a case of providing vehicles and locomotives for all these special trains. Stops had to be scheduled for refreshments, at places where a *division* of hearty Americans could be satisfied. Other trains had to be diverted, or side-tracked. I wonder how many readers will have memories of that memorable BBC feature broadcast *Junction X*, which told in the most vivid detail how Crewe dealt with a sudden change in the programmed routeing of a convoy of trains from an arriving ship from the North Atlantic. At the time of the actual broadcast the identity of Junction X was of course not revealed, but the programme researcher did his homework very thoroughly in and around Crewe.

CHAPTER 12

Ebb Tide — Nationalisation

The last shots against Nazi Germany had barely been fired and the immediate danger to the British Isles removed, before the wonderful unity that had held our nation together in its darkest days began to disperse. The war in the Pacific was likely to go on for some time, but at home Parliament had run long beyond its normal statutory span, and Winston Churchill, like the good Parliamentarian that he was, decided that the time had come for a general election. At once all the worst features of party politics were let loose. The Labour members of the War Cabinet resigned, and men who had toiled together unceasingly since 1940 were soon flinging mud at each other across the hustings. Our 'finest hour' had gone. The result of that general election in which Churchill, to quote his own words was 'dismissed by the British electorate', and which stunned the rest of the world into virtual disbelief, made one thing certain, the railways of Britain would soon be nationalised. To many people, despite the political sentiments manifested by the overwhelming result of the election, this prospect brought some very mixed feelings, but to those who had railways at heart, some very disturbing trends began to be apparent.

During the war everyone, service personnel and civilians alike were prepared to put up with any inconvenience while travelling. There were certainly some, who had hardly, if ever, used the railways in pre-war years, and who were distressed that petrol rationing denied them the use of their cars in the later stages of the war. Introduced to long distance railway travelling when the conditions were the worst in history, they were not impressed! The fact also that many months were to pass after Victory Day in May 1945 before there was any sign of improvement tended to give the impression that excessively crowded trains, slow and late running, and the most primitive arrangements for obtaining refreshments, were the normal way of travelling by train. The attitude of some others, not necessarily motorists in pre-war days, was summed up by a middle-aged man of my acquaintance, when he heard that nationalisation was likely: 'The railways', he declared, 'had made such a mess of it that it was about time someone else had a go'! The experience on which this pronouncement was made had, of course, been entirely as a passenger. The staggering achievements in freight haulage during the war, touched upon no more than briefly in the previous chapter would be quite unknown to him. But that attitude was unfortunately all too common in that time-honoured, but quite unrepresentative individual, the 'man in the street'.

Some of our former allies were more discerning in their appraisal of the railway situation in Great Britain at the end of the war. An eminent Dutch engineer, on one public occasion, emphasised how the rolling stock and fixed equipment of our railways had been worked almost to the point of complete collapse, yet still continued to give a marvellously comprehensive service. Coaching stock was certainly dirty, the majority of locomotives still dirtier, and track maintenance routines had necessarily been extended far beyond standards that would have been permitted in pre-war years. In 1939 one could not have imagined a train on the West Coast main line, of all routes, becoming derailed on a straight stretch, because of the state of the track! Coal supplies were erratic. Output from the British mining industry, also in process of being nationalised was inadequate, and considerable tonnages were being imported in 1946-7. Could one have foreseen a situation when a local train in South Wales would be halted several times between stations with its engine short of steam, through being fired on American coal—in South Wales! The Great Western Railway, in its last years of independence, fitted a number of its locomotives for oil firing, and as if to emphasise the difficulties put some of them to work in South Wales. Railways had never in their history been favoured with a friendly press, and when the bill for nationalisation was introduced into the House of Commons some of the statements made by men whose appointments under the Crown should have induced at least some sense of responsibility just took one's breath away.

That the Minister of Transport in Clement Attlee's Government had no previous experience in transport went almost without saying. The Bill he presented, and eventually steam rollered through Parliament was a purely political measure, and inevitably received strong opposition from the great majority of men who had held positions of high responsbility on the railways in their independent days. Lacking so completely any previous knowledge of transport, the Minister naturally sought help and co-operation from senior railway management; but from some, whose counsels would have been invaluable, resignation was chosen instead. Also, a great bank of highly responsible experience was cast on one side. It was, I suppose, not to be expected that a Government of such political faiths would have consulted many of the former railway directors, who in the shibboleths hurled from the hustings were regarded as so many parasites. That the majority of senior railway officers did co-operate, and strove loyally to build up a new national organisation in the spirit of the measure passed through Parliament is a matter of history, even though many who were left in the regional organisations did not approve of the appointments made to the central co-ordinating body, the Railway Executive, which reported to the supreme authority, the British Transport Commission.

The only railway officer to be appointed as a full time member of the BTC was Sir William Wood, formerly President of the LMS. This caused some heart-searching elsewhere, because he was by no means the most senior in years of service among the top executives of the former main line railways. Sir James Milne of the GWR, who had been deputy chairman of the REC during the war, was offered the chairmanship of the Railway Executive, but he declined, and choice then fell upon Sir Eustace Missenden, formerly General Manager of the Southern. The executive posts in the new organisation were parcelled out among officers of the former railways thus:

V. M. Barrington-Ward (LNER) operating;

David Blee (GWR) commercial;

R. A. Riddles (LMS) mechanical and electrical engineering;

J. C. L. Train (LNER) civil engineering and signalling.

The Railway Executive was completed by General Sir William Slim, a distinguished soldier, and W. P. Allen, a former engine driver, representing trade union interests. For a company of its former status the Great Western was but thinly represented; it was understood that membership of the executive responsible for civil engineering and signalling was in the first place offered to Allan Quartermaine, Chief Engineer of the GWR, but was declined.

At this distance in time I may perhaps be permitted to record a personal impression, formed from contact with a number of them, made in the carrying out of a literary commission, and that is that the senior officers of the GWR took the whole process of nationalisation very badly; while co-operating in the early discussions towards the new organisation they seemed unwilling to take major responsibility beyond the confines of their own system. Whether this could be traced to Sir James Milne's refusal to take the chairmanship of the Railway Executive I cannot say. Under the various members of the executive, among the Chief Officers appointed from January 1948 a high proportion of those responsible for operation and engineering came from the former LMS:

CO Operating (HQ) S. E. Parkhouse (LMS);

CO Operating (Eastern Group) E. W. Rostern (LNER);

CO Motive Power H. Rudgard (LMS);

CO Loco Construction & Maintenance R. C. Bond (LMS);

CO Carriage & Wagon Construction and Maintenance E. Pugson (LMS);

Chief Electrical Engineer C. M. Cock (Southern);

Chief Officer Engineering (Works) A. Dean (LNER);

Executive Officer (Signals and Telecommunications) H. H. Dyer (LMS);

Executive Officer, Engineering Development R. C. Rattray (LNER);

Executive Officer, Locomotive Design E. S. Cox (LMS);

Chief Officer (Goods) J. R. Pike (LMS);

Executive Officer (Mineral Traffic) D. Murray (LNER);

Executive Officer (Terminals) A. C. B. Pickford (GWR);

Chief Officer (Continental) R. H. Hacker (Southern).

It was clear from the above appointments that operating practice was going to be standardised on the Midland-LMS pattern. Barrington-Ward had previously adopted this in the Southern Area of the LNER, and with Parkhouse, Rostern, and Col Rudgard (ex-Midland) in key positions it was likely to be extended on a national basis. In locomotive design and construction the position appeared to be solid LMS, though Riddles himself was most anxious to avoid giving preference to the practices of his old company without the most searching examination of the practices of the other three companies. Very soon after 1 January 1948 Lord Hurcomb, Chairman of the BTC, asked Riddles what colour he was going to paint the locomotives and was taken by surprise at the uncompromising answer he got: 'black'! The noble lord replied: 'Oh, come; you can't do that', and a parade of locomotives painted in various colours was staged at Addison Road station. It was thought undesirable to perpetuate any one of the pre-nationalisation liveries so several experimental styles, including a dark blue reminiscent of the Great Eastern, were tried for the largest express passenger engines, and pale green for the second line classes, such as Royal Scots, Castles, and Lord Nelsons. Both this green and the experimental dark blue were set off by a style of lining strongly savouring the old LNWR, which was emphasised by the choice of the Crewe livery, virtually unchanged, for the mixed traffic engines. Even after Lord Hurcomb's mild admonition, Riddles made one final attempt to get black by instructing Crewe to paint one of the Princess Royal class 4-6-2s in full LNWR livery. Neither the dark blue nor the pale green stayed. For a time the Kings and the express passenger Pacifics were painted in Caledonian blue, but with black underframes; eventually Great Western green became the standard BR livery for passenger engines.

Far more important than liveries was, of course, the major question of standardisation—not only of locomotives, but of fixed equipment, operating practice, and all administrative matters. One of the claims made for unification of the railways, under national ownership, had been the economies that could be effected, by a single standard, nationwide. Railway enthusiasts eagerly awaited any developments in this direction so far as locomotives were concerned, but in principle this was one of the easiest areas to attack. Far more fundamental differences in detail existed in operating practices, which included signalling, and I would not attempt to probe into the problems of accounting, stores, and general administration in which the newly established Regions differed so much from each other. In signalling and operating practice the first months—indeed years—of nationalisation were spent by the headquarters' staffs collating details of existing practice and details of equipment. It was a tremendous task, and for some time there was no sign of any unified practice emerging. The Regions just carried on. There was another factor that began to intrude most seriously upon all ideas of equipment standardisation—a virtual freeze on capital expenditure. In the simple and obvious case of semaphore signals the Great Western had stood alone in its retention of the lower quadrant type; but to have ordained that all these should be forthwith brought into line with the majority would have been an expensive matter, quite apart from the partisan feelings it would have aroused.

So far as locomotives were concerned, there was a strong feeling from the very outset that we should follow the American example and get rid of steam traction as soon as possible. Riddles took a strongly different view. Diesels would involve importing far more oil than the nation could then afford. Furthermore they were much more expensive, and he announced his policy in very simple terms: 'We're going to have the form of traction that provides the most tractive effort *per pound sterling'* — in other words home-built steam. In the economic climate of that year of railway destiny, 1948, it was undoubtedly the most prudent course. It delighted the railway enthusiasts but depressed the industrialists. The policy to be adopted in locomotive standardisation had many aspects to be considered. The practice and designs of one of the former companies could have been adopted in toto. Riddles and his two senior lieutenants R. C. Bond and E. S. Cox knew very well that they had, on the LMS, locomotives that were ideal for national standards. The Great Western, though a first-rate fleet, would have been unacceptable from the loading gauge point of view, and since the death of Sir Nigel Gresley, the image of LNER motive power had become rather tarnished. The Southern, pursuing a policy towards electrification in pre-war years, had relatively few modern engine designs except the controversial Bulleid Pacifics.

To have taken LMS practice would, however, have been psychologically unsound, and when the interesting series of interchange trials between express passenger, mixed traffic, and freight locomotives conducted in the spring and summer of 1948 showed that none of the regional types had a sufficiently marked advantage over the others to justify its adoption as a national standard Riddles embarked upon the fairest, but most difficult policy of all, to work out a series of new national designs that would embody all that was best in the regional types. The interchange trials of 1948, and the decision to evolve new standards were to have remarkably beneficial effects in bringing the staffs of the former railway companies into co-operation with each other. At the outset it can well be imagined that the process of nationalisation went very much against the grain in proud, hitherto autonomous locomotive establishments like Derby, Doncaster and Swindon. A man who, as Chief Mechanical Engineer of the GWR, had the responsibility for running, as well as for design and construction, and a staff of more than 20,000 men, and on the other hand a man of the individuality like O. V. S. Bulleid, would not have taken kindly to yielding their autonomy to a central engineering authority. To their lasting credit it may be said that whatever they may have felt none of the former CMEs rocked the boat of the Railway Executive.

It was no more than natural, however, that it was to their assistants, as the men of the future, that Riddles and his own staff looked more intently; the interchange trials and the design policy that followed brought many of the younger men into close contact. Not only was a design team, chaired by E. S. Cox, set up to establish the principles and details to be embodied in the new locomotives, but no fewer than five main locomotive works were entrusted with the detail design of various components and with the erection of the finished locomotives. In this way Brighton, Crewe, Derby, Doncaster and Swindon all took a hand. While there might have been disadvantages in that each particular class was not the product of a single works and its associated drawing office, the whole project was based upon teamwork throughout; that is what Riddles set out to achieve, while at the same time producing a range of sound, economical locomotives. It was significant, however, that the first locomotive of the new standard range did not take the road until three years after the interchange trials.

While the introduction of the new locomotives was one of the most spectacular manifestations of nationalisation, several important projects, the completion of which had been postponed by the war, were brought to fruition in the early years of nationalisation, and added notably to the strength of the

British railway network. One of these was the electrification of the former Great Central main line between Manchester and Sheffield, with the very important connection to Wath hump marshalling yard. At the time this was authorised, the system of electric traction recommended for the future standard on British railways was 1500 volts direct current, in keeping with contemporary development in France. And the Manchester-Sheffield project was completed at the same time as the French were electrifying the former PLM main line from Paris, southwards towards Lyons. The electrification of the Manchester-Sheffield line involved the tremendous civil engineering task of boring a new Woodhead Tunnel, double-tracked, parallel to the two existing single-tracked bores, and causing the civil engineers of the 1940s just as much trouble as the original bores had extended all Joseph Locke's ingenuity and resources a hundred years earlier!

Two major signalling schemes brought into service in the earlier years of nationalisation, contributed notably to the operating facilities of the east coast main line, yet showed variations of operating philosophy even within what was formerly a single company, the LNER. They exemplified the divergences in signalling and operating practice that the Railway Executive had ultimately to solve, if a completely standard code of practice was to emerge eventually. The two installations were at Doncaster and York, respectively in the Southern and North-Eastern Areas of the former LNER. Doncaster was a one-off. There was never another one like it before or since. It was one of the brain-children of that most inventive and original signal engineer, A. E. Tattersall, and Doncaster was an expression of the principle of sequence switch interlocking. But from the operating point of view the way it differed from the great installation at York was in having two signal boxes, one at each end of the station. This reflected a philosophy of operation that had unexpected bedfellows on British Railways. In the Southern Area of the LNER Barrington-Ward was one of its advocates, preferring

156

the two-box conception, and he, in pre-war days, had been the operational architect of Doncaster. The Great Western had also followed it consistently in the big power installations it had commissioned in the 1930s at Paddington, Bristol and Cardiff.

It was the North Eastern Area of the LNER, however, that was setting the pattern of the future in its combination of panel signal boxes with an operating philosophy that favoured large single concentrations of control, and the opening of the large central signal box at York in 1952 was one of the greatest milestones in British railway history in the twentieth century. It is true that the form of panel, and the detail process of setting up routes has developed on somewhat different lines, but the operational principle was established, to be vastly extended to the great advantage of traffic regulation on the principal major routes of the country when, by electronic remote control methods, the geographical areas covered by such panel signal boxes could be immeasurably enlarged to cover long sections of main line.

CHAPTER 13

Modernisation — GO-STOP-GO!

It would have been very surprising if the organisation set up initially to carry through so vast a change as the nationalisation of the British railways had been right first time. Political opponents of the Government that set it up were ready enough to criticise, and when a Conservative administration took over, in 1952, it seemed that changes were inevitable. There was even talk of repealing the Act of 1947 which had established nationalisation. It was felt, however, that a central administration that gave greater freedom of action to the Regions was desirable. In giving expression to such sentiments, however, there was introduced the first of several measures changing the structure of the 'centre', as it had become known, and creating uncertainties and frustrations for those who had the highest and most responsible tasks. In 1953, the two-tier organisation of the British Transport Commission, and the Railway Executive reporting it, was replaced by an interim organisation in which a 'General Staff' was interposed between the Commission and the Regions, and a distinguished soldier, Sir Brian Robertson, was appointed as the next chairman of the BTC.

Hamstrung as it had been by the financial difficulties of the Labour Government elected in such enthusiasm in 1945, the Railway Executive had not been able to do more than scratch the tip of the iceberg so far as standardisation was concerned. It was felt on all sides that a massive injection of new capital was needed. British railwaymen saw with dismay the rapid strides which European networks were making towards wholly modern installations, while our own, with halting and

Above: One of the British Railways standard 7MT Pacifics of the Britannia class No 70027 *Rising Star* on the up Red Dragon South Wales to Paddington express near Reading. *(M. W. Earley)*

Below: A scene on Beattock bank, in 1964: a Manchester–Glasgow express hauled by one of the Class 40 diesel-electrics (then numbered D317) passes a down freight, berthed in the siding at Greskine box. *(Derek Cross)*

Above: The new Euston in 1972; 100mph electric trains IH42 for Manchester and IS75 for Glasgow, hauled by electric locomotives of Class AL6 (now known as Class 86). *(Derek Cross)*
Below: The high-speed era: Inter-City 125 HST diesel-electric unit on the East Coast main line, passing Durham. *(British Rail, ER)*

uncertain steps was apparently condemned to make do and mend. Yet railways like those of France and Holland had been bombed almost to a standstill in the closing stages of the war, and now with generous financial aid from outside seemed to be striding far ahead of us. In Great Britain much was blamed on our retention of steam as the principal form of traction, and when the new standard locomotives introduced in 1951 got off to a rather shaky start the anti-steam lobby, both inside and outside the railways themselves redoubled their advocacy of a change. The Government of the day took up the cause, not on behalf of traction alone, but in sponsoring general modernisation; in 1955, there was launched the great Modernisation Plan.

It included, within the £1200 million voted by Parliament, a limited degree of main line electrification; the extension of the Southern Region electric network; the complete elimination of steam traction; a large allocation of capital for modern colour-light signalling, and the building of a number of large new marshalling yards at key points of major traffic concentrations. The purposes of the latter was to eliminate untidy, wasteful and time-consuming processes of shunting, often in a number of small yards that had grown up piecemeal over the long years in which the railway network had gradually developed. A further very important feature of the plan was to equip a large number of freight wagons with continuous brakes, as a first step towards removing the anomaly of the loose-coupled freight train. So far as traction was concerned, on non-electrified routes it was envisaged that diesel locomotives would replace steam for main line haulage of both passenger and freight trains, and that on lightly used branch lines diesel railcars would take over. With this overall policy, as announced when the broad outlines of the Modernisation Plan were published, Riddles was not in agreement. He contended that the capital made available for traction improvement should be expended on electrification in clearly defined geographical areas, and steam traction, of which many

161

thousands of efficient units were still available in 1954, and were a long way short of their economic life, should be concentrated elsewhere — in much the same way as was happening at that time in France. There should be no intermingling of the systems of traction. But he was overruled and he resigned in consequence.

Traction apart, however, British Railways as a whole launched on a spending spree without parallel. It was a very anxious time for railway engineers in every discipline. In embarking upon a novel course of action their judgements based upon long experience counselled caution, and asked for time in which new methods and equipment might be given appropriate trial. But capital having been made available the placing of contracts was regarded as a matter of top priority, in no area more so than in the replacement of steam locomotives by diesels. The financial situation was going from bad to worse, and the 'scrap steam' faction was becoming ever more vocal. With a naivety that in retrospect takes some believing that faction repeatedly expressed their conviction: 'We shall be all right once we're rid of steam'. The engineers recommended that a first investment should be made in 164 main line units, in capacity ranging from 800 to 2000 horsepower; and then, for a period of three years no further additions should be made until there had been a proper opportunity to give these pioneer designs a thorough trial. But although this recommendation was accepted at first it was soon overruled, and contracts for bulk purchases of locomotives placed. They were received before servicing and maintenance facilities had been prepared, and in many cases had to be accommodated in steam sheds, with inevitably disastrous results.

An equally serious situation developed over the fitting of continuous brakes to freight trains. Faced with the situation that much of the existing coaching stock, as well as locomotives, was due for replacement, and that large orders were to be placed for new wagon stock, the engineers recommended that the nettle should be grasped, and the long overdue change from vacuum to air brakes should be made as part of the modernisation plan. There was of course no question of the technical superiority of the air brake particularly for higher speeds. There would, of course, have been a period of inconvenience while the transition was in progress, but at the speed aimed at for conversion from steam to diesel traction, with all the problems anticipated, a change in the type of brake would have almost been incidental! The operating staff, however, persuaded the BRB that the difficulties of transition in brakes were more than they could stomach, and so the vacuum brake remained—for a few more years. Far worse was the situation that developed over the fitting of vacuum brakes to freight wagons. Contracts were placed simultaneously, for large numbers of new wagons, and for the brake equipment. In one case a company to whom a contract was awarded had to set up a special manufacturing facility to meet the volume and urgent delivery with which equipment was demanded, only to have this plant thrown first into idleness and then redundancy because the complementary activity proved completely unable to fulfil manufacturing requirement at all.

In signalling there was little standardisation at first. Each region had to accept what the manufacturers could supply in the limited time available. Naturally in such circumstances there was some jockeying for position to try and get this or that design accepted as a future national pattern, but one of the most striking changes in style of signalling control was that on the Southern. In that area, over the years, modern power signalling practice had become more nearly standardised than anywhere else in Great Britain, using miniature-lever interlocking frames, and electric lever interlocking. Throughout the former Southern Railway, technologists and signal inspectors were thoroughly conversant with the well-established techniques; new installations, no matter how large, or how complicated the track layout were treated almost as a matter of routine. From 1954 onwards principles entirely new

163

to them had to be learned. The Great Western, now the Western Region, adopted button/switch control panels with relay interlocking for the first time and showed its individuality by use of the domino type of console, hitherto marketed by a Swiss manufacturer.

The Chief Electrical Engineer of the British Railways Board also had second thoughts about the system of electric traction to be adopted, and the decision to change from 1500 volts direct current was taken entirely on the strength of French experience. Trials of 25,000 volts (25kV) alternating current at the commercial frequency of 50 cycles per second (50Hz), had shown such advantages in first cost of the overhead equipment, and greater efficiency in working that the SNCF had decided to change for the future. So far as standardisation was concerned, the SNCF was far more heavily committed with existing installations on the 1500 volt dc system than we were in Great Britain, so that their decision to change had been fraught with many more pros and cons than anything facing the BRB. The responsibility for making the change in the UK was that of S. B. Warder, then Chief Electrical Engineer, and it was a decision over which there has since been no cause to regret.

Before the electrification of the London Midland main line southwards from Liverpool and Manchester to London, including in its final stage the very busy loop main line north-west from Rugby, through Coventry, Birmingham and Wolverhampton to rejoin the principal main line at Stafford, had progressed very far there was a major crisis. One is too near to the decade of the 1960s to be able to give a reasoned, balanced commentary upon the events that shook British Railways during those anxious years. The personalities are too vividly in mind: Ernest Marples, Barbara Castle and her several successors, with the Ministry of Transport turned upside down; at the BRB, after Robertson there came and went Beeching, Raymond, Johnson—the only true railwayman —and Marsh, down to the present chairman Sir Peter Parker.

To use a popular word of today, it was traumatic—traumatic for everyone, railwaymen of all grades, for the supply services, for the travelling public, who never knew what to expect next, and for those who the French so happily call 'friends of the railway'.

As for the enthusiasts, countless of them had been horrified when the motive power on their favourite branch lines had been changed from small steam locomotives to diesel railcars, but when Beeching sought to close down many of them altogether their sentiments, for totally different reasons, became at one with local residents and traders. The latter joined forces in mighty protest at the prospect even though they rarely used these branch lines; when indignation meetings were organised, in certain cases the arguments against closure were not exactly strengthened when some of the most vociferous travelled to these meetings by road transport. In all the circumstances it is remarkable that so much *was* done by way of modernisation. Beeching's mandate had been clear enough, to make the railways pay, and he set about it in a logical and statistical manner by proposing to close down all those activities that did not pay. His activities at one time went to the extent of stopping work on the electrification of the London Midland main line from Euston, because it was felt that the results would not give an adequate return on the capital invested. There were so many issues involved in this one single project, and urgent representations were made by senior railwaymen that postponement would increase the eventual costs, by interfering with the planned flow of work, and involving higher costs when the component parts were taken up again, and restarted. A very disturbing feature of some current thought was that no appreciable acceleration of train service would be necessary after completion. The mere change to electric traction would be enough to win back lost traffic. However all was well in the end, and in May 1966 what, in another book, I called 'Britain's New Railway' was brought into supremely spectacular operation.

The adjective 'new' was no mere catchword to give the electrification of the London Midland main line from Euston an initial boost. It *was* a new railway—new in everything except the routes it followed. A new railway had been built over the routes of the former LNWR. To sustain the tremendous usage of a swarm of electric trains thundering down the line, all at 100mph or near it, the roadbed had to be completely rebuilt. The formation was renewed; new and much deeper ballasting was laid, and the track itself, heavy flat bottomed rails, continuously welded and carried on reinforced concrete sleepers, was the finest that had yet been seen in Great Britain. This rebuilt line was equipped almost throughout with four-aspect colour-light signals so spaced that the 100mph expresses could follow each other at 3-minute intervals, if need be. Splendid new panel signal boxes were installed, concentrating the control of traffic flowing in a wide area into a single room in each case, from which the regulation of train movements could be efficiently monitored and organised to the best advantage of all classes of train. The former London & North Western Railway, although providing one of the most lavish and punctual passenger train services in the country, was never famed for the elegance of its stations, and as part of the new era Manchester, London Road, as it used to be known, was given an extensive face-lift from the public image point of view, and had its track layout modernised. Euston and Birmingham New Street stations were completely rebuilt.

It was sad that in the very thorough modernisation of Euston, that transformed it from a jumble that had grown with the years into one of the finest terminal stations anywhere from the traffic operating point of view, that no way was found of incorporating into the new complex the famous Doric Arch. It would have formed so magnificent a centrepiece, a focal point for the whole modern traffic complex. It is to be hoped that its less known, and less spectacular counterpart, at the other end of Robert Stephenson's London & Birmingham

Railway, the classic entrance to Curzon Street, now the goods terminal, will be preserved for posterity.

With the tremendous upsurge in passenger traffic following the opening of the electrified line throughout from London to Liverpool and Manchester, it was hoped that authority would soon be forthcoming for its extension to Glasgow, because the organisation and resources were immediately available, and could be switched on to the new work with minimum additional capital cost for plant and so on. But unfortunately it did not happen that way. Many years were to pass before the signal changed from 'stop' to 'go', and by then, of course, the constructional plant had been disposed of, technical staffs of both contractors and British Railways switched to other work, and in the meantime costs in every quarter had risen steeply. When the line was eventually electrified through to Glasgow, in 1974, it had cost much more than if it had been done immediately after the London-Birmingham-Liverpool-Manchester project had been completed.

After the decision had been taken to adopt the 25kV ac 50Hz electrification system, there was considerable discussion as to how the projected conversion of the Southern Region line to Bournemouth, to electric traction should be treated. The line to Portsmouth, electrified in 1937, had taken the third-rail, low voltage direct current system as far down the main line from Waterloo as Woking, and the same system had been used for the Kent Coast lines. But so far as Bournemouth was concerned serious consideration was at first given to installing the 25kV ac system beyond Woking, even though the inconvenience of changing systems at Woking would have been involved. This would not have been an insuperable difficulty in itself, because dual voltage traction locomotives were then in use in France. But a major factor lay in the need to provide the through service from Waterloo to Weymouth, as a continuation of the Bournemouth run, and the line beyond Bournemouth was not to be electrified. Multiple-unit trains of the usual Southern type could therefore not be used, and the

Weymouth sections would require diesel haulage beyond Bournemouth.

To avoid the inconvenience of locomotive haulage on the electrified part of the line, and with it obviating the need for light engine working at Waterloo, an ingenious solution was attained by use of a single power unit, embodied in what is termed a four-car tractor unit, known by the code name of 4REP. The motor bogies under these sets have a total of 3200 horsepower, and on the busier services the tractor unit propels two four-car trailer units on the down run, the leading cab of which is occupied by the driver. On arrival at Bournemouth the leading four-car unit is detached, and taken forward to Weymouth by a diesel-electric locomotive. This is equipped for push-pull working, so that on the up journey the four-car set is propelled to Bournemouth, and there coupled up to the electric train. The driving trailer cars are so equipped that they can control either the 4REP tractor units, when working down from Waterloo to Bournemouth, or a diesel-electric locomotive when being propelled up from Weymouth to Bournemouth. These arrangements provided a very smart new service on this line from July 1967.

The electrification of the West Coast main line, northward from Weaver Junction to Glasgow, was a much deferred project. The vision was there even before the Manchester-Liverpool-Euston scheme was completed. Farsighted railwaymen, top ranking in all the necessary disciplines, saw the way ahead clearly enough, but of course those who controlled the national finances could not be expected to put the same emphasis on railway modernisation. And the 'stop' period was a long one! The British Railways Board made its submission of the case for this extension of electrification to the Government in April 1968, and then a great silence descended upon the whole scene. The Prime Minister of the day chose that particular moment to change the Minister of Transport, replacing Richard Marsh by Fred Mulley. Nearly two years elapsed during which time many people had given up hope that the electrification project would be authorised. Then, on 23 February 1970, the welcome news came through, and in May 1974 the full electric service between London and Glasgow was inaugurated.

CHAPTER 14

Into the High Speed Age

The almost incredible speed with which the first phase of British railway modernisation was carried out created some very mixed feelings, not only within the railway service and its supporting industries, but especially among the large body of friendly support within the general public — young and old. Among the latter especially it was the positively shipwreck hurry in which steam traction was eliminated that caused the deepest emotional and partisan sentiments; but the swiftness of that metamorphosis, the completion of which was very nearly reached by the years 1965-6, created for British Railways management problems for the future that were of the utmost importance. An entire fleet of new motive power had been introduced in a very short time, within the decade 1955-65, and it would fall due for renewal in the late 1970s and 1980s. The way in which this should be renewed presented British Railways with the task of making some difficult decisions having regard to a diversity of influencing factors.

It was the matter of Inter-City travel that posed the more difficult questions, such as, what was the market likely to be in 10 to 20 years' time; how would competitive forms of transport have developed, and what would technology have to offer by then? It is important to appreciate that in facing the problem British Railways management had to be thinking some ten years in advance of the time when replacements would become necessary. In any considerations towards the future development of Inter-City service five major points constantly had to be borne in mind:

1 Journey time: the need for high *average* speed;
2 Frequency: to match as near as possible the convenience of a private car;

170

3 Safety: in the search for higher speed, there could be no reduction in safety standards;

4 Reliability: the standards of reliability must be maintained, or even enhanced;

5 Amenities: seating comfort, a good ride, minimum noise, attractive catering.

From experience in the electrified London, Birmingham, Liverpool, Manchester service, there was no doubt that higher speed, coupled with the other four factors listed above, paid off handsomely. In the four years following completion, and thus some time before the extension to Glasgow was in operation, there had been an increase in passenger journeys of 100 per cent; a passenger survey carried out to try and find out why showed that between 40 and 50 per cent of passengers using the high speed electric trains did so because the journey time was the quickest and the least tiring. At the same time an assessment of the competitive market showed that railway travel was highly competitive with all other forms up to a journey time of three hours, with the overall time between London and Liverpool and London and Manchester occupying a little over 2½ hours. For journeys longer than three hours, as the overall time increased there was a progressive loss of business to the air. At the same time the massive constructional programme of a national motorway network was introducing strong competition for Inter-City journeys between 100 and 180 miles. Improvements in both road and air transport within Great Britain were likely to increase, and it was clear that the railways would be able to sustain, or improve their share of the market only if improved facilities could be offered. With the level of maximum speed on the principal main lines already up to 100mph it seemed clear that improved services would require significant technological advances, and with the time scale for major change of product being up to 10 years, from conception to widespread implementation, decisions had to be taken in the early 1970s.

A dominant factor in any considerations for major accelera-

171

tion of passenger train services in Great Britain is that the railway system serves a densely populated island, and that very little of the existing network was designed with really high speeds in mind. Much of the route mileage has a high percentage of curves which limit maximum speed. Even in the case of the four principal trunk routes, namely West Coast London to Glasgow, East Coast London to Edinburgh, London to the West Country and South Wales, and the North East to South West cross-country route, on only two of them was a substantial part suitable for high speed without extensive alteration. It is true that in the course of modernisation when the traction was being changed from steam to diesel and electric the massive improvements in track and signalling made the lines suitable for higher speed without much additional work, but having regard to what had been done in Japan, and what was even then contemplated in West Germany and France in building entirely separate new lines to provide high speed Inter-City service, British Railways carried out a study to determine whether a similar investment would be justified to connect London with any other of the major industrial centres. In a country such as ours, which is compact, highly developed and densely populated, it was concluded that no case could be made, within the strict financial criteria applied to any new investment, for the construction of such a new line or lines.

So the whole of technical research was directed towards making better use of the existing network, and this research, while leading into two quite distinct studies has resulted in projects that are basically related in the overall strategy of passenger train improvement on British Railways. The first involved the use of established technology, and modern improvement in power and vehicle design to produce a train known as the High Speed Train capable of running at 125mph and having improved braking characteristics so that complete reconstruction of the signalling and control systems would be unnecessary. Such a train would enable substantial acceleration of service to be made on a limited number of routes, where improvements could be carried out economically; elsewhere, because of the high percentage of curves, the improvement in time likely to be effected by the use of such trains was less than ideal. The second possibility was to develop an entirely new train, embodying new technologies that would enable curves to be rounded safely and comfortably at much higher speeds, and thus to permit substantially higher *average* speeds on curved routes. The unknown factor in this case was the time likely to be taken to achieve technological success in an entirely new product, and its ultimate cost, measured against the likely increase in revenue from the shorter journey times predicted.

The choice before British Railways in the early 1970s was difficult, whether to go for a modernised High Speed Train, giving promise of much faster services on no more than a few routes, or to take a chance on a new technology offering much more general advantages, if successful, but greater risks of achievement, in the Advanced Passenger Train. The outcome was a characteristic British compromise, in which the BRB opted to take advantage of the suitability of each type of train for specific routes, investing in the HST for a limited number where its potentialities could be most readily exploited, and to press ahead with the development of the Advanced Passenger Train. Experimental work on the APT was already encouraging, and it was necessary to seek assurance that the beneficial features would be confirmed in a limited number of pre-production trains. The original intention was that the Advanced Passenger Trains would be gas-turbine propelled, while the High Speed Trains would be diesel-electric. By 1972 the prototype HST had been complete, and after objections by ASLEF to its crewing had been overcome driver training took place early in 1973, and some high speed trial runs were made in June. On one of these a maximum speed of 143mph was attained between Northallerton and Thirsk. I was one of a party invited to make a trip in the train from King's Cross to

Darlington and back on 2 August 1973, and on the return trip the 44.1 miles from Darlington to York were covered in 27min 37sec start to stop, including a maximum speed, near Thirsk, of 137mph.

After the period of trial running and this public demonstration of its capacity for speed with its exceptionally smooth riding, British Railways received the necessary financial authority to go ahead towards the introduction of a full HST service. The route chosen for this first application was the one on which the track could most readily and economically be rendered suitable for continuous running, over lengthy mileages, at 125mph — that of the former Great Western Railway, engineered by I. K. Brunel from Paddington to Bristol, together with the South Wales main line. Both were traditionally well patronised services, and with the High Speed Trains giving promise of substantially reduced journey times from London to Bath and Bristol, on the one hand, and to Newport, Cardiff and points west on the other, the investment seemed a profitable one to pursue. In regular service the new trains were to be limited to a maximum speed of 125mph but the magnificent alignment of this original Brunellian route, and no less that of the South Wales Direct line from Wootton Bassett via Badminton, made it possible, with relatively little additional work, to permit the maintenance of 125mph continuously over lengthy mileages. It should be emphasised of course that during the first phase of modernisation on British Railways, from 1960 onwards the permanent way had already been brought to a very high standard of maintenance, permitting speeds up to 100mph, while the multiple-aspect colour-light signalling provided adequate braking distance from that speed, with locomotive-hauled trains.

One of the most essential requirements in the equipment of the High Speed Trains was the provision of brake power that would ensure smooth stopping from 125mph in the same distance that the existing locomotive hauled trains could stop from 100mph, thus obviating any need for changes in signalling. Sufficient of the new HST sets, incorporating improved features found desirable from the running of the prototype of 1972-3, were available for new, greatly accelerated services to be introduced on the London-Bristol, London-South Wales routes from October 1976. Since then progressive improvements to the track have enabled minor limitations in maximum speed, below 125mph, to be removed and further small accelerations have been made. At the time of writing, on Brunel's original main line the fastest scheduled times to Bath (106.9 miles) and Bristol Temple Meads (118.3 miles), are 70 and 87min, inclusive of one and two stops respectively, and giving overall average speeds of 91.8 and 81.5mph. The latter average is reduced not only by the inclusion of two intermediate stops, but also by the provision of some recovery time in the short concluding run between Bath and Bristol. Certain of these trains make their first stop at Chippenham, covering the 94 miles from Paddington in 57min, an average speed of 99.2mph from start to stop.

In introducing these HST services, the exceptionally favourable track conditions of the London-Bristol route, and that from London to South Wales as far as Bristol Parkway station were appreciated, and that it would be impracticable to achieve such radical improvements in journey time on more than a few other routes in the country. The programme of new locomotive and coach construction agreed in the mid-1970s envisaged the use of diesel-electric HST sets on only three others, namely the East Coast main line, between London, Edinburgh and Aberdeen, on the West of England main line between London, Exeter, Plymouth and Penzance, and on the cross-country North East to South West route, from Newcastle via Sheffield, Birmingham and Bristol, to Exeter and Plymouth. Except in the case of the East Coast main line south of Edinburgh, it was realised that the improvement in overall average speeds could not be so spectacular as those achieved on the first two Western Region routes. Nevertheless on the main line through Cornwall, for example, the tractive power built into the HST sets would enable the severe inclines to be climbed at speeds almost comparable to the maximum permitted *downhill*, and with rapid recovery of speed from the various permanent restrictions some significant acceleration would be possible.

Since the completion of the electrification of the west coast main line, a very important and convenient connectional pattern of train services was established at Birmingham, with no more than a cross-platform interchange between trains on the North East — South West, South Wales axis, and trains to Liverpool, Manchester and Scotland northwards and southwards to Oxford, Southampton/Bournemouth. There are various permutations on the theme but as an example, trains from Bristol and the West of England, and from South Wales follow each other at close headway from Gloucester to Birmingham, whence one proceeds to the North West and the other to the North East, having made cross-platform connection with each other in Birmingham. The projected introduction of HST sets on the North East to South West route will make possible some useful Inter-City accelerations, because there are sections of this line on which 125mph running will eventually be permissible, as between Derby and the outskirts of Birmingham, over parts of the line southwards to Bristol, and certainly over the Brunellian main line between Bristol and Taunton. A great deal of the passenger business on this through route is from point to point, involving relatively short journeys, evidenced by the large interchange of passengers at such stations as Derby, Birmingham and Bristol.

HST sets were introduced on the East Coast main line in the summer of 1978, providing services between King's Cross and Newcastle, 268.3 miles in 3hr 5 to 18min, with a highest average speed of 87.5mph and a hitherto unparalleled time of 4hr 52min to Edinburgh by the Flying Scotsman. At first the HST services did not proceed north of Edinburgh, but it is the ultimate intention to continue certain of them through to Aberdeen. The prospects of a general revision of East Coast timetables, with the full quota of HST sets were unhappily baulked by the catastrophic collapse of the roof in Penmanshiel Tunnel, between Berwick-on-Tweed and Dunbar, early in 1979, which completely severed main line railway communication between Berwick and Edinburgh. The planners and civil engineers though acted with remarkable speed and a completely new length of railway was built as a deviation avoiding the tunnel and brought into service in August 1979. Now the HST sets are providing the same immaculately smooth and rapid service to which travellers on the Western Region have become accustomed. A typical example is a run about which I have details of the 07.40 down from King's Cross, which after calling at Stevenage to pick up passengers from the outer residential areas of London, ran the 160½ miles to York in 106min, making a start-to-stop average of 91mph though hindered at three points because of engineering work on the line.

Meanwhile development of the Advanced Passenger Train was proceeding. In 1970 it was decided to build an experimental train uniquely with gas-turbine power to prove the technological innovations included in its conception. This train had a designed maximum speed of 155mph but from the commercial angle its potentialities were more clearly shown in an experimental run from St Pancras to Leicester on which the 99 miles were run in 58½min. The minimum time of ordinary locomotive-hauled trains over this route is about 80min; but the tilting mechanism of the APT, providing a high degree of sensitivity to curves to allow faster running round curves with no passenger discomfort, enabled the average speed of the run to be increased from 74 to 101mph. Following this successful experimental work, construction of three pre-production electrically powered APT sets was authorised in 1974, for running on the west coast main line between London and Glasgow.

So while the diesel-electric HST sets are providing a spectacular improvement in overall journey speed on the few routes where their attributes can be fully exploited, the indications are that the train of the future for the *general* improvement of Inter-City passenger train services over the whole country is the APT, which of course can be built either for electric or diesel propulsion, according to the equipment of the routes to which sets are allocated. The London-Leicester test run is a clear indication of the possibilities, and indeed of the *requirements* of the future, when start-to-stop average speeds of at least 100mph will be the standard, rather than the exceptional Inter-City service on British Railways, despite the curves and complexities of this intense railway network.

CHAPTER 15

Britain's Gift to the World

Although this account of how main line railways began, grew and prospered has concentrated on Great Britain and Ireland, it must never be forgotten that railways were a wholly British invention, the knowledge of which was passed on to other countries. Of course if the term rail-ways is taken in its broadest sense, as relating to any form of transport in which a vehicle runs on a guided track, whether the motive power is horses, gravitation, or even—as in Australia—convict push-power, there were rail-ways in many parts of the world before the Liverpool & Manchester line was projected, but this latter was the first Inter-City railway intended to carry passengers in large numbers, as well as freight, and it is as such that its sesquicentenary celebrations were planned for 1980. The impact of the Liverpool & Manchester was such that its effect soon spread abroad. This final chapter recalls the extent to which this British invention has been applied and adapted to the benefit of inland transport in nearly every country on earth. The main line railway could indeed be described as 'Britain's Gift to the World'.

Rainhill was not only a personal triumph for the Stephensons but a tremendous boost for the new means of transport, and very soon afterwards British engineers were consulted by European countries on the building of railways, and the provision of motive power for them. Stephenson-built locomotives hauled the first trains in Belgium, Germany, and Russia, while George Stephenson's historic line across the wastes of Chat Moss provided the inspiration for that great Dutch engineer, Conrad, in carrying the first railway in the Netherlands over the largely undrained marshlands that had

179

to be crossed in building the line from Amsterdam to Rotterdam. All the same the great new profession of mechanical engineering was still in its infancy, and more than seventeen years were to pass before public recognition came with the founding of the Institution bearing its name, with George Stephenson as the first president. It is remarkable, however, that despite this initial lack of recognition British practitioners began to achieve such worldwide fame.

In the USA and Canada local conditions were against the standardisation of the early British types of steam locomotive, though in France, a British type, the Crampton rear-driver, won far more general acceptance than at home. The influence of the Liverpool & Manchester Railway became very strong for a time in North-West France. Joseph Locke and his famous contractor Thomas Brassey built the Paris & Rouen line and carried it further west; largely at Locke's suggestion W. B. Buddicom, Locomotive Superintendent at Edge Hill, Liverpool, relinquished his position there to set up a locomotive manufactory in France, primarily with the idea of supplying locomotives to the railways Locke and Brassey were building. 'Le Buddicom' for a time became as familiar a feature on the early French railways as did the Crampton type in other areas in France. In railway planning and construction, Robert Stephenson was consulted on the first main line railway in Switzerland, running through the relatively level central valleys from east to west and linking Basle and Berne with Lausanne and Geneva; his outline proposals for an initial network north of the Alps were largely carried out in due course. Brunel was consulted on the early Italian railways.

In most countries that were eventually knit together to form the British Empire, it was natural that inspiration and expertise came from the mother country. In an early chapter of this book, mention was made of Lord Dalhousie's presidency of the Board of Trade at the time of the gauge war. Shortly afterwards he was appointed Governor General of India at a time when the affairs of that sub-continent were administered in a general way by the East India Company. Dalhousie drew up a scheme for a network of main line railways, planned with two major considerations, firstly defence, at a time when the North West Frontier was regarded as the greatest danger point from outside attack, and secondly the development of trade, carrying the greatly sought products of India to the ports for shipment to Europe. In the gradual build-up of the network that Dalhousie planned, the financing, civil engineering, and operational know-how was entirely British.

In North America the building of railways was at first a matter of colonising, and with very little capital available the lines were constructed as cheaply as possible, avoiding major constructional works, taking river-level routes wherever possible, and following tortuous alignments in many areas. This precluded the general adoption of the European type of steam locomotive, which had been developed to suit massively built, relatively straight and easily graded lines. But the Civil War brought both a tactical and strategic significance to railways in America. The style of tracks and rolling stock were ideally suitable for rapid repair and restoration of traffic after hostile attack, but President Lincoln realised the great potential danger that lay in the isolation of the west coast settlements from the Great Lakes area, and the eastern seaboard; under ministerial decree the building of a trans-continental link was hastened forward. It was the first truly classic instance of the projection of a railway through virgin, almost uncharted country to consolidate and unify a nation.

About 20 years later, two great Scots and their tremendous American colleague William Cornelius Van Horne did the same for Canada. The provinces lying beyond the Rocky Mountains were at first not enthusiastic about joining the Dominion, and just as Lincoln had felt at the time of the American Civil War, so the Canadian Prime Minister, John A. MacDonald, sensed that if a more tangible unity with the west was not achieved there was a danger of them breaking away, and in all probability becoming part of the USA. Appreciating that their feeling of isolation was largely due to lack of good communication with the east, MacDonald promised that if British Columbia became a part of the new Dominion a railway would be built, linking them with the prairie provinces. British Columbia took the bait, and came in, but the construction of that railway was more easily promised than achieved. The building of the Canadian Pacific Railway is one of the greatest romances in the transport history of the world, though while it was in progress one can be very sure that the great, indefatigable trio who carried the burden of responsibility had little thoughts of romance themselves! The trio consisted of Donald A. Smith, afterwards Lord Strathcona, George Stephen, a fellow and equally indomitable Scot, and Van Horne. The completion of the task, in 1885, was one of the greatest milestones in the history of Canada, and it was King George V, when Prince of Wales, who once said: 'We have seen how the Canadian Pacific Railway has helped to make a Nation'.

A closely parallel case arose in Australia in 1901. The eastern states of that extraordinary continent sought to consolidate the hitherto separate colonies into a single commonwealth, and like British Columbia, the colony of Western Australia, separated from the rest by vast stretches of unpopulated 'nothing', and having no means of communication except by sea showed some preference for remaining independent. Again the enticement of a transcontinental railway was offered, and again it had the desired result. In Australia, however, there was a serious complication, that of rail gauges. After the experience of the gauge war in England one would have thought that a similar situation would not have been permitted to develop elsewhere, particularly in Australia, where at first the infant colonies were under the direct control of Parliament in London. Indeed when railways were first projected almost simultaneously in New South Wales, Victoria and South Australia, each colony, in turn referred the matter of the rail gauge to the home Government.

They all got the same reply, in words to this effect: 'We do not mind what gauge you adopt, as long as all three of you are the same'.

First in the field was New South Wales, with an Irish engineer, with the name of Shields. He no doubt, out of loyalty to the railways of his homeland proposed a gauge of 5ft 3in; Victoria and South Australia agreed, and London approved. Construction started, and rolling stock was ordered from the United Kingdom. But then Shields had a violent disagreement with the Government of New South Wales and resigned. His place was taken by a Scotsman, Wallace by name, who immediately reversed his predecessor's recommendation and insisted that the British gauge of 4ft 8½in should be used. Unfortunately no one thought to tell Victoria and South Australia, and by the time they heard of this change of policy they had ordered locomotives and rolling stock, and roundly declared it was too late to change. At that time of course the lines of communication between the Australian colonies were very slight, and news travelled but slowly. Thus it came about that when the state railways of New South Wales and Victoria advanced stage by stage to their frontier on the Murray River, at Albury, there was a break of gauge. In Queensland, when railway construction began the colonists gave no thought to the eventual linking of their pioneer tracks with those of New South Wales and arguing that they could get a much greater mileage of railway for the same money by building on a narrower gauge than 4ft 8½in they decided upon 3ft 6in Western Australia did the same, and so the Commonwealth got *three* gauges!

When the time came for implementing the promise to Western Australia to provide a railway to link them with the eastern states the question naturally arose as to what the gauge should be, with 3ft 6in at one end, and the 5ft 3in of South Australia at the other. The Commonwealth Government took the farsighted view that one day there would have to be a unification of gauge in Australia, and 4ft 8½in was decided

183

upon. Thus the long line across the great emptiness of the Nullabor Plain was built to that gauge. When it was completed in 1917 there were breaks of gauge at each end, but after a very long interval a new 4ft 8½ in gauge link was constructed from Kalgoorlie to Perth partly as mixed gauge combined with 3ft 6in, and eventually in 1970, a new line was constructed eastwards from Port Pirie, South Australia, to link up with the New South Wales system at Broken Hill and so provide a 4ft 8½ in gauge line right across Australia.

British engineers built railways in South America, Japan, and China; but one of the grandest and most imaginative of all projects was that of Cecil Rhodes. By his magnificent conception of a Cape to Cairo Railway, a conception unhappily never to be consummated, he hoped to do for the entire African continent what the Canadian Pacific had done for Canada, and what the trans-Australian line was eventually to do in the land of the Southern Cross. But Africa, ethno-logically, politically and strategically was very different from Canada and Australia. There were wars against local potentates in Egypt and the Sudan, in South Africa rival colonial interests rent the country, and successive wars left a legacy of suspicion, distrust, and deep seated antagonism not only between races, but between the European factions. It is remarkable that in the circumstances so much was done to build trunk lines of railway even before the end of the nine-teenth century: from the Cape to the gold mining areas of the Reef; in the Sudan, and in the remote country to the west of the Transvaal where, with the vigour of Cecil Rhodes' enterprise the Cape to Cairo line was driven northwards in Rhodesia.

The Cape to Cairo project died hard. In a brochure of 1930 issued by the Benguela Railway there was a map titled 'Africa showing the Benguela Railway in relation to Cape-Cairo and other rail routes', and this had printed on it the proposed line linking up the southernmost point on the Sudan Government Railways with those of the Belgian Congo, at Stanleyville. The

184

gauge, except in Egypt, was 3ft 6in and the manner in which the technology of steam locomotive engineering was developed to provide some of the most powerful locomotives in the world on that gauge, was one of the unfolding phenomena of the railway world from the 1920s onward. Not only on the Cape to Cairo line, but on others built by British engineers in Africa the alignments had necessarily to be tortuous in wild jungle and mountainous country to avoid excessive constructional costs. At first, in South Africa, an attempt to meet the need for locomotives of exceptional power was made by introduction of the Mallet compound type of articulated locomotive, which at the beginnings of the 1920s had attained popularity in the USA. But a notable series of trials on a sharply curved and heavily graded section in Natal, in 1921, showed without any doubt, that the British engineered Beyer-Garratt type of articulated locomotive was vastly better than the Mallet in such running conditions, and it proved another British 'gift to the world', many of which are still working in Southern Africa today, at a time when the steam locomotive is reaching the end of its life.

One of the most remarkable among the pioneer colonising railways of Africa, built by British engineers, was the Uganda. Splendid in its conception, dramatic beyond measure in the tactical details of its survey and construction, it recalls the jocular description once applied to Canada as 'a country 3000 miles long and two railroads wide'! Certainly the railway 550 miles long from Mombasa to Port Florance on Lake Victoria Nyanza, completed in 1903, proved the lifeline and focus of subsequent development in the territory then known as the British East Africa and Uganda Protectorate. To build this line British engineers, relying for their work-force almost entirely upon coolies imported from India, worked in a countryside that was almost trackless, one huge expanse of jungle, swamp and desert. The working parties had to be protected by escorts armed to the teeth, while night after night the dense jungle surrounding the encampments resounded with the trumpeting of elephants, the roaring of lions and the war cries and tom-toms of savages.

*   *   *   *

By way of an epilogue, and at the extreme opposite end of the speed scale in what Britain has presented to the world, I must mention the great record in start-to-stop average speed made by a British passenger train in the very week that I was writing this chapter, when one of the HST sets described in the previous chapter ran the 94 miles from London (Paddington) to Chippenham in 50min 32sec, without exceeding the official maximum speed limit of 125mph. This impressive world record was made over the line engineered by Brunel, more than 140 years ago, and is yet another resounding tribute to one of the greatest of those pioneers to whom we are today indebted for the foundations of the British main line railway system of today. Moreover the HST could find a place in the railway history of countries beside Britain, for they are being looked at by other administrations as possible contenders for high-speed air-conditioned luxury units for the 1980s.

Bibliography

Histories, definitive and detailed

Britain's New Railway O. S. Nock Ian Allan
The Centenary History of the Liverpool & Manchester Railway
C. F. Dendy-Marshall Locomotive Publishing Co 1930
Great Central Railway Vols 1, 2, 3 George Dow Ian Allan
History of British Railways during the War, 1939-45 R. Bell
The Railway Gazette 1946
History of the Great Northern Railway Charles H. Grinling
George Allen & Unwin 1966
History of the Great Western Railway Vols 1 & 2 E. T.
Macdermot Vol 3 O. S. Nock Ian Allan New Edition 1964
History of the North Eastern Railway W. Tomlinson reprint
David & Charles 1967
History of the Southern Railway C. F. Dendy-Marshall Ian
Allan 1963
The Midland Railway: Its rise and progress New Printing of
1876 work F. S. Williams David & Charles 1968
Newcastle & Carlisle Railway John S. Maclean R. Robinson &
Co 1948
Railway Race to the North O. S. Nock Ian Allan 1959

Historical Studies

Caledonian Railway O. S. Nock Ian Allan 1962
Great Eastern Railway Cecil J. Allen Ian Allan 1964
Great North of Scotland Railway H. A. Vallance David &
Charles 1963

187

Highland Railway O. S. Nock Ian Allan 1962
Lancashire & Yorkshire Railway O. S. Nock Ian Allan 1969
London & South Western Railway O. S. Nock Ian Allan 1966
Narrow Gauge Railway of Ireland H. Fayle Greenlake Publications 1946
North Western O. S. Nock Ian Allan 1968
South Eastern & Chatham Railway O. S. Nock Ian Allan 1961
West Highland Railway John Thomas David & Charles 1965

General Books

British Railways in Transition O. S. Nock Thomas Nelson & Sons 1963
British Steam Railways O. S. Nock A. & C. Black 1961
Our Home Railways W. J. Gordon Frederick Warne & Co 1910
Railway Engineers O. S. Nock B. T. Batsford 1955
The Railways of England W. M. Acworth reprint (originally published 1899) Ian Allan

Index